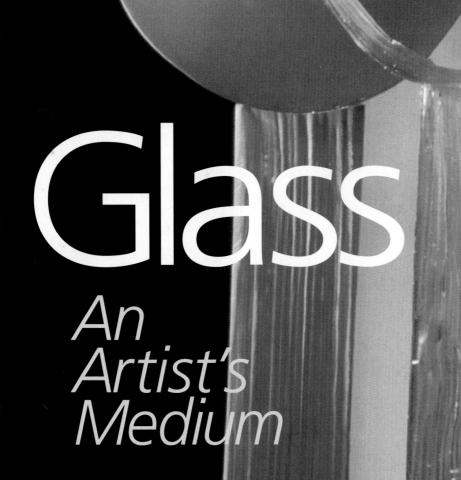

Glass

*An
Artist's
Medium*

Lucartha Kohler

Published by

 krause publications
700 E. State St., Iola, WI 54990-0001

Please, call or write us for our free catalog of antiques and collectibles publications. To place an order or receive our free catalog, call 800-258-0929. For editorial comment and further information, use our regular business telephone at (715) 445-2214.

Library of Congress Catalog Number: applied
ISBN: 0-87431-604-x
Printed in the United States of America

Acknowledgments

I wish to thank Wheaton Village and all of the artists who so generously shared their information and work for the book, as well as many technicians who have helped me over the years, including Dr. Frank E. Woolley and the Studio of the Corning Museum. Thanks especially to Marvin Lipofsky who helped and encouraged me early on to write the book and to persist in seeing it through. Thanks also to Bill Happel for being there (sometimes) when I needed help, information, tools and supplies. And many thanks to all of my students who helped me explain what I know, and to Sid Sachs who helped me write what I explained.
To my family.

–Lucartha Kohler

Preface

Glass is a miracle material, an inorganic liquid arrested in a state of rigidity midway between aqueousness and crystallization. At certain temperatures, it can be pulled, poured and pounded without losing its physical integrity; at others, it can be sawed, drilled, sliced, etched, abraded, cracked and even pulverized. When molten, new glass can be added on anywhere and will fuse like "Flubber" or "Silly Putty." Even when cold and hard, if you cut it, the cut can heal itself. This is one of the fascinating things I learned reading this book, which is full of vital information on every way of working with glass (except glassblowing). Blowing glass remains essentially a team effort, despite the rhetoric of the so-called "Studio Glass Movement," and the author's focus is on artists like herself working alone in their studios who use or want to use glass as their material.

Lucartha Kohler goes against the tradition of secrecy she cites as the hallmark of glassmaking throughout its history–she tells all. Glass's 5,000-year history and its properties serve as a background to her descriptions of how hot glass is formed in furnaces by blowing and casting teams, how warm glass is lampworked and kiln-formed in the studio, and how it is cold-worked in a myriad of ways. She gives precise recipes and formulas, equipment lists (with tips on how to make-do with items from the kitchen or garage) and describes each process in detail, using artists known for their work in that area as focal points for the discussion. Tricks, such as how to find out how much glass you have to put in a mold to be sure it will be full when it melts, are interspersed with warnings about health hazards and essential safety precautions.

The author's 25 years of learning to manipulate her material coincided with a veritable explosion in its popularity among artists and art students, dealers and collectors. Glass is so versatile, so useful and unabashedly decorative, so protean in nature, it may be the cyborgian material of the future. Kohler has condensed her experiences with the material and her familiarity with the other artists using it into one surprisingly easy-to-read, information-packed volume. She takes traditional shop and industrial techniques, which have been developed over the centuries in team situations, into the artist's studio for solo performances.

–April Kingsley
Former curator of the American Crafts Museum

Table of Contents

Introduction

Glass is unique among all other materials used in the creation of art. The uniqueness of glass exists in all of the specific qualities that are inherent in the material, plus the aura of mystery that surrounds its historic traditions. As a material it can be clear and transparent, as if non-existent, or it can be dense and opaque like metal or stone. An object made from glass can be sensual and beautiful or it can be downright ugly. It can also be thought-provoking and inspirational or physically threatening and even dangerous. Glass is a hard and rigid chemical compound, but it is not a solid, it is a rigid liquid, at once setting it apart from other materials.

From its beginnings, the procedures and formulas used in glassmaking were shrouded in mystery. The craft of glassmaking was passed from father to son and, later, from master to apprentice. Formulas and techniques were closely guarded; at times, in history, the penalty for betrayal was death. Despite difficult circumstances, glassmaking spread to all of the known world. Each distinct geographical area had a unique design-vocabulary strongly influenced by its cultural heritage.

For centuries, the development of glass technology and glassware design was a gradual evolution. Major stylistic advancements were slow to be absorbed into the body of technical knowledge; individual artists were rarely acknowledged. The Industrial Revolution began the shift away from the hand-making of glass. This change was swift and dramatic in the United States. Glass became a product for packaging, building and consuming. The handwork tradition had little to do with these new products. The process of industrialization affected the process of handmaking as a few artists in Europe and America discovered earlier in this century. Modern industrial technology could be scaled down to a personal level, as Harvey Littleton, an artist, and Dominic Labino, a glass technician for Johns-Manville Glass Co. in Toledo, Ohio, proved by building a glass furnace on the grounds of the Toledo Museum in 1962. As a result of that workshop, artists could continue the ancient traditions with contemporary knowledge, tools and equipment.

Industrialization, mass-production and the revival of the ancient craft have presented new insights into the nature of what a handmade glass object can be. Is it art? Is it craft? Is it neither? Or both? These questions are perplexing. The very same set of values applicable to all created objects, whether they are made from paint, wood, stone, clay, metal, plastic, fibers or some ethereal substance, applies to objects made from glass. Because of the inherent difficulties surrounding the execution of a glass object, craftsmanship is often inexorably intertwined with its conception. Rapidly changing trends in the art world have led to acceptance of the aesthetic value of objects traditionally associated with craft materials.

This century, a relatively short period of time in the history of art, has seen radical changes in the evolution of sculpture. From sculpture's traditional heritage as architectural adornment, park monument and portraiture, has emerged the three-dimensional object. Dada, Surrealist, Pop Art, Modernist and Postmodernist labels all contribute to the new vocabulary of object as sculpture and, therefore, art. One factor that has influenced the trend away from traditional sculptural techniques has been the accessibility of industrial materials and computers for both execution and design. Today's artist has a limitless supply of materials and concepts. The only constraints are aesthetic criteria and the language of design.

The purpose of this book is to present information regarding technical aspects of glass as they relate to artistic practices. Some of the techniques included are from industry, some are from architectural applications, but most are from the long tradition of glass as applied design. All of the artists' included in this book work with glass as either part or all of their work. To some artists, the way of working is more important than the why of working. To other artists the work exists apart from the forming process. While yet, to others, the inherent properties of the material dictate their forms.

I came to glass from a background in traditional sculpture techniques. I knew how to model in clay and wax, work directly in metal by welding, soldering and brazing. I was experienced in bronze casting techniques, mold making, and I even worked some in fired ceramics. To me, the material was just a way to make my art. I thought I had a handle on things until I fell in love with that elusive, mysterious, magical material–glass.

This book is a result of many years of trial and error–a quest to know more about the material and how to make it do my bidding. I learned that the material has a will of its own and the best I could do was encourage it along my way. Through this long process, I learned a great deal about patience, persistence and the Zen of kiln maintenance.

Glass art today is as diverse as the ways glass can be used; some of the results have been very exciting. The full potential of glass as a material for artists, however, is just beginning to be explored. It is impossible to cover all aspects of glass working in one book. I hope you will use this as a guide book to embark upon a magical journey through "The Looking Glass."

–Lucartha Kohler

Section 1

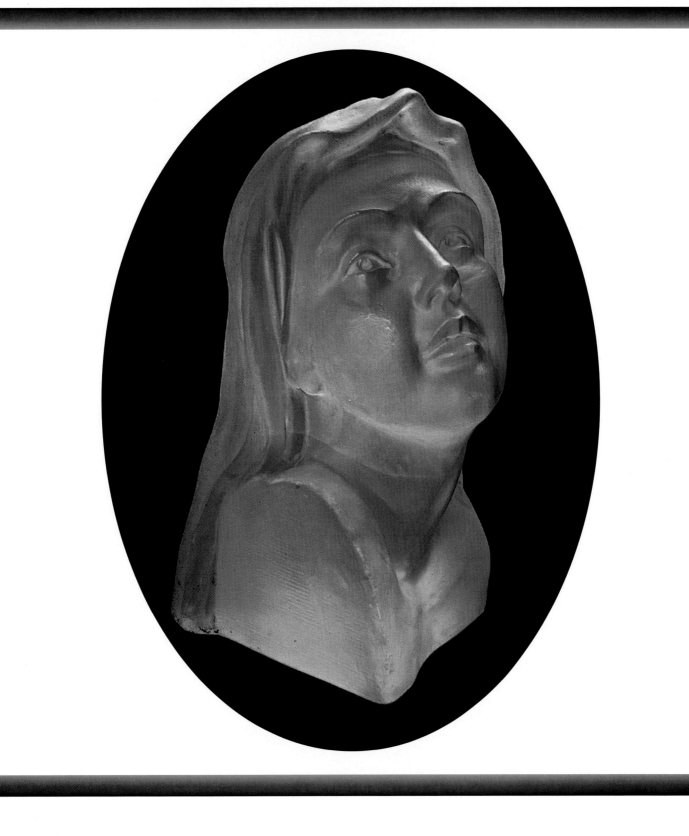

History of Glass: The First 5,000 Years

There remains glass, the preparation of which belongs here, for the reason that it is obtained by the power of fire and subtle art from solidified juices and from coarse or fine sand, it is transparent, as are certain solidified juices, gems and stones; and can be melted like fusible stones and metals. First I must speak of the materials from which glass is made; then of the furnace in which it is melted; then of the methods by which it is produced.

Agricola, 1556[1]

The early history of glass is obscure and shrouded in mystery; however, somewhere in the Middle East around 5,000 years ago someone first made glass; either by accident or by design. Many legends tell of its discovery. Although none of the existing tales have any factual evidence to support them, it is believed by many to have been the Phoenicians from Caanan who first created glass. Caanan was a land along the Eastern Mediterranean where modern Lebanon and Israel are located today. The Phoenicians were merchants and seafaring people and quite possibly spread their glassmaking knowledge throughout the known world. The most popular account is told by Pliny, the Roman historian, who, according to rumor, had an explanation for everything known in the first century AD.

He writes: "The tradition is that a merchant ship laden with nitrum (soda and potash) being moored at this place, the merchants were preparing their meal on the beach, and not having stones to prop up their pots, they used lumps of nitrum from the ship, which fused and mixed with the sands of the shore, and there flowed streams of a new translucent liquid, and thus was the origin of glass"[2]

If, in fact, there is a grain of truth to this tale, humankind's curiosity perhaps led to investigation, duplication and control of this incredible discovery.

Pendant, New Kingdom 18th Dynasty, 1400-1360 BC, Amenhotep II, Egypt, 3.7 cm long x 1.5 cm wide x 7 mm thick, 59.1.91. (photo courtesy of The Corning Museum of Glass)

Glass bead neck-lace imitating carnelian, agate, amethyst, marble and turquoise, Roman first to third century AD, 83.231. (photo courtesy of the Newark Museum)

Beads Are Earliest Remnants

The earliest glass remnants found to date are beads. Glass beads could have been produced in the Middle East or Egypt as early as the third millennium BC. Glass in the form of a glaze for pottery was known to the Egyptians prior to 3000 BC. Most specimens remaining today date from the New Kingdom around 1500 BC. Glass beads were made by winding a thin thread of molten glass from a clay pot or crucible around a wire core. Egyptian beads were highly prized by other cultures and were traded like gold and precious stones. Blue beads were especially desirable, for they were thought to possess magical powers. Even today, throughout the Middle East, Greece and Turkey, blue eye beads are thought to be magical and are worn to ward-off evil spirits.

The recorded history of glass begins with the New Kingdom in Egypt. In addition to beads, the Egyptians made ointment jars and perfume bottles formed by the core-formed method. A mixture of dung, clay, sand and water was fastened to a metal rod. Molten glass threads were wound around the core and continually reheated to fuse the threads together. After the glass cooled, the rod and core were removed. Almost from the beginning, intricate glass rods or canes were formed by layering colors of glass

Core formed Kohl tube in shape of a lotus column, 14th-12th century BC, 50.1239. (photo courtesy of the Newark Museum)

9

in elaborate patterns. These rods were cut up and used as precious stones in jewelry and other forms of body adornment.

The early Egyptians also used glass to make objects and architectural adornments. Statues, reliefs and mosaics were made by the casting method, thought to have evolved from metal casting techniques well known at that time. By the second century BC, they had developed a method of fusing glass rods into intricate millefiori mosaics and bowls that were highly prized throughout the Roman Empire.

During the first century BC, glass centers appeared all around the Mediterranean. The Syrians probably blew the first bubble, although there is little evidence to support this as fact. Both the Egyptians and Syrians were known to make solid rods and hollow tubes in glass. Quite possibly, the discovery of glassblowing began with one of these tubes. Perhaps the end of a heated tube melted and closed off. The glass worker forced air through the tube and a bubble was formed. We will never know for sure, but all blown glass since then starts as a bubble.

The Syrians were possibly producing glass as early as the Egyptians; however, the distinct style of Syrian glass did not emerge until much later. The most significant advancements in both decorative and functional glassware have been attributed to the Alexandrian Egyptians. They were influenced by the Greek Hellenistic decorative style and the skills of the Syrian craftsmen.

Statuette of Venus first to second century AD Roman Empire, 9.4 cm high x 4.3 cm wide. 55.1.84. (photo courtesy of The Corning Museum of Glass)

Mold-blown opaque white head flask, first century AD 87.79. (photo courtesy of the Newark Museum)

Glass Was Highly Valued

Glass centers flourished in scattered areas throughout the Roman Empire. Rome itself had a few glass houses, but was never a major glass center. However, powerful Roman Emperors did encourage and support the manufacture of glass objects. The value of some of these objects equaled that of precious stones and metals. The vast realm of the Empire and the territories covered by the Romans through conquest and trade introduced glass objects as far north as Scandinavia and the British Isles, and as far east as China. The decline of the Roman Empire by the fifth century AD forced glassmakers to relocate. Many settled in the Rhine valley to the north and developed the distinct heavy Bohemian style of glassmaking, while others went east to Byzantium where glass became delicate and highly decorative. Eastern glassmakers developed surface decorating techniques such as enameling, staining and gilding with gold and silver, and European glassmakers developed decorative motifs within the molten glass.

Medieval Europe, as documented by Theophilus in *The Divers Arts*[3] and Agricola in *De Re Metalica*[4] was well known for creating both functional glassware and colored glass for windows. Both of these manuscripts contain instructions for working with glass. The medieval alchemist, father of modern chemistry, found that glass flasks were important tools for his experiments. The miraculous transformation of earth (sand) into glass, by fire, was in itself an alchemical transformation.

The art of glassmaking was kept alive by Muslim artisans throughout the vast Islamic world. Elaborately decorated Byzantine glass was highly prized, and cargo ships carried it as far away as China. Theophilus, in his medieval treatise on painting,

Mold-blown Ennion Cup, first century AD, signed in Greek "Ennion made me," 50.1443. (photo courtesy of the Newark Museum)

glassmaking and metalwork, discusses the influence of Byzantine glass on European craftsmen. The chapters "Glass Goblets which the Byzantine Embellish with Gold and Silver" and "Byzantine Glass which Embellishes Mosaic Work"[5] explain in some detail how to fire glassware with gold and silver lusters, as well as mixing ground pigments for painting on glass.

The Venice Glassmakers

Glassmaking was introduced to Venice during the Byzantine period by craftsmen from Constantinople. The industry grew so rapidly that the large numbers of glass houses posed a threat of fire to the city. During the 11th century, all of the shops were moved to the nearby island of Murano, where glassmaking prospered and the tiny island reigned supreme as the glass center of all the known world. The formulas and techniques of the Murano glass houses were a closely guarded secret.

The master glassmakers of Venice were rewarded for their skill by appointment to the court; however, even as noblemen, they were virtually held prisoner on the island. The mastery of their craft was rivaled only by their creative invention. Among their inventive accomplishments were goblets, bowls and novelty items deco-rated with complex, intricate lattachino designs within the molten glass. Another invention that became very popular was artificial pearls. These pearls were made with an external surface coating on fine hollow-blown beads. In addition to the delicately blown glassware,

Byzantine gold glass tile, sixth to 12th century AD, 72.138. (photo courtesy of the Newark Museum)

there was a demand for both glass mosaic pavements and clear and colored window glass, by both churches and wealthy noblemen. The ability to produce a clear and colorless glass, combined with metallic plating or gilding, led to the creation of looking glasses; these mirrors soon became popular all over Europe with the ladies of the courts.

In France, glassmakers developed a means of casting large plates of glass for looking glasses. Louis XIV was an ardent patron of the glass industry; through his generous support, great strides were made in the technical development of plate glass for windows and mirrors. The Hall of Mirrors at Versailles and many other large plate-glass mirrors manufactured during his reign, still remain.

Throughout Europe, from the 13th to the 16th century, practical inventions popped up as a result of the mass appeal of glass. In England, during the latter part of the 13th century, the philosopher, Roger Bacon, invented spectacles using ground glass lenses. A Dutchman, Anton Van Leeuwenhoek, supposedly made the first ground lens. Thus, microscopes and telescopes were developed and became popular devices for looking at all manner of small things.

Hall of Mirrors, Versailles Palace, France. (photo by the author)

Over the centuries, the quality of glass increased in clarity and the technical expertise developed to melt many new colors. This made the material desirable for popular household items, as well as stained glass windows in many sacred shrines. In 1674, the addition of lead to the glass formula by an Englishman, George Ravenscroft, produced a soft easily cut and engraved, brilliant glass suitable for the most noble table.

Engraved panel depicting Adam and Eve with the tree of knowledge, circa 1650-1675, Europe, possibly Germany, colorless glass, blown polished, engraved. 23.1 cm high x 18.7 cm wide x 0.2 cm thick, 87.3.1, gift of Lucy Smith and Clara S. Peck. (photo courtesy of the Corning Museum of Glass)

Lampworking Introduced

Around the same time that lead was introduced, lampworking (the melting of glass in the flame of a lamp), seems to have been in common use. Robert Hooke, in his *Micrographia*, 1665, mentions the use of the lamp for flameworking: "And hence it is, that if you take a very clear piece of a broken Venice Glass, and in a Lamp draw it out into very small hairs or threads, then holding the ends of these threads in the flame, till they melt and run into a small round globul, or drop, which will hang at the end of the thread."[6]

The use of a flame to melt glass was mostly limited to scientific applications until the late 19th century when the Blaschkas, a father and son from Bohemia, developed a technique to make realistic botanical glass models. Petals, leaves and stems, were painstakingly rendered separately in clear glass in the heat of the flame. Colored glass was finely ground into powders and then carefully painted onto each part of the flower. After many layers of painting, subtle colorations and fine detail, the individual part was refired in the flame to permanently set the colors. Upon completion of all of the parts, the flowers were assembled. The entire collection is housed today in the Ware Collection of Blaschka Glass Models, the Botanical Museum, Harvard University. "Rudolph Blaschka expressed regret that many people thought that his handiwork utilized secret processes; he insisted that his work represented art in which there is no room for secrecy or egoism."[7] No one has even made an attempt to reproduce the Blashka's technique since that time.

As the sciences became more inquisitive and the scientific method more demanding of specialized equipment, lampworking became a highly skilled craft in the service of science, limiting the use of a flame to make art until very recently.

The great Crystal Palace Exhibition in 1851 brought about many changes in design theory. The Victorian era saw lavish decoration on everything from tableware to architecture. William Morris, an English designer and father of the Arts and Crafts movement, rebelled against such ornate decor, believing in the importance of function and the presence of the human heart and hand in all crafted objects.

Coneflower, Blaschka Flower. (photo courtesy of the Botanical Museum of Harvard University, Cambridge, MA, photograph by Hillel Burger)

Art Nouveau in Style

By the end of the 19th century, French glassmakers were giving the Venetians a run for their money and showing the English a thing or two about style. Art Nouveau, a movement affecting all of the arts, saw design move toward nature and expression of the inner soul. A group of artists from Nancy, became known as the Nancy School and were the most influential.

Emile Gallé, son of a glassmaker from Nancy, was skilled in the glassmaker's craft, as well as educated in the arts. As a member of the Nancy School, he applied his efforts toward Art Nouveau design in glass. His work enjoyed enormous success and influenced many including Antonin Daum, son of the founder of Daum et Cie, Cristallerie de Nancy. Young Daum produced very fine examples of Art Nouveau design in glass and continued to experiment with innovative styles and techniques, including *pate de verre*.[8]

Henry Cros, "Portrait of Caroline Hill," about 1900, France, pate de verre, 30.5 cm high, 66.3.17. (photo courtesy of the Corning Museum of Glass)

Another Frenchman, Henri Cros, first produced a technique he called *pate de verre*. His interest in ancient Roman and Egyptian colored-glass sculptures led him to research the techniques used by these early craftsmen. He experimented with ground glass mixed with a binding agent. His first glass medallion was melted in his kitchen oven. Pleased with his success, he built a kiln in his workshop and continued to produce reliefs and medallions. As is the case with most creative spirits, his projects became more and more ambitious. In 1894, he completed his first large panel "L'Histoire de L'eau." In 1900, a second panel "L'Histoire de Feu" was completed and is now in the Museum of Decorative Arts in Paris.

At the same time, unknown to Cros, another Frenchman, Georges Despret, was also experimenting with ground glass to create sculptural forms. His life's work remained concentrated on the execution of small sculpture in *pate de verre*. Both men remained very secretive about their techniques. Most of the technical information from these and other glass workers of that era has been lost.

Glass in America

In comparison to the long and illustrious history of Old World glassmaking, the history of American glass is brief but flamboyant. In a few hundred years, American glass technology

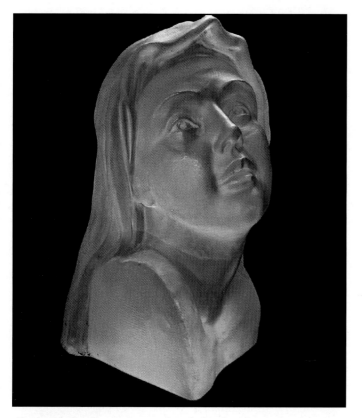

Frederick Carder, sculpture, female head with scarf, cast using lost wax method, gift of the maker, 52.4.332. (photo courtesy of the Corning Museum of Glass)

has developed by leaps and bounds. From very crude beginnings, some handmade glass objects have attained the stature of fine art. One man responsible for that success was Frederick Carder. In 1903, Carder was brought from Stourbridge, England, to steer the newly formed Steuben Glass Works in Corning, New York. Steuben was founded to supply the growing interest in art glass begun by Gallé, in France, and Tiffany in America. In 1934, when at the age of 70 he retired from his position as head of design at Steuben, Carder began experimenting with casting glass. His approach to casting involved the *cire perdue* (lost wax) method of casting often used by metal foundries. He was familiar with the *pate de verre* work of the French glassmakers, but their information remained obscure. Determination led to success. His most ambitious attempt was to cast an 800-pound Indian head. The piece was cast with Corning Pyrex. To Carders' great disappointment, the piece cracked as it was removed from the mold. Unlike his predecessors, Carder was very open about sharing his information. His notes and formulas have helped many others with a desire to cast glass, including myself.

Edris Eckhardt, from Cleveland, Ohio, began experimenting with glass in the early 1950s. Although her background was sculpture and ceramics, she was fascinated by ancient Roman glass and began extensive experiments to discover their techniques. This work earned her a fellowship from the Guggenheim

Foundation and a Tiffany Foundation Award. In the 1960s, she began to execute *pate de verre* sculptures in the lost wax technique using what she referred to as a ceramic shell investment.[9] A number of major museums have her cast work in their collections, but the major focus of museum interest in glass until recently has been blown objects.

There were others during the 1950s and early 1960s who were experimenting with kiln-formed processes. Maurice Heaton and Frances and Michael Higgens were painting with enamels and slumping with some very interesting results. The current interest in kiln-formed glass has brought about new interest in the work of some of these early pioneers.

Daum et Cie, also in the 1950s renewed their earlier interest in *pate de verre* and worked with a number of well-known artists of the time to execute their works of art in glass. Salvador Dali was one of this group. That practice continued well into the 1980s to include works by Dan Dailey.

References

1. Agricola, Georgius, *De Re Metallica*, translated by Herbert Clark Hoover and Lou Henry Hoover, Dover Publishing.
2. See 1.
3. *On Divers Arts*, translated by John G. Hawthorne and Cyril Stanley Smith, Dover Publishing.
4. See 1.
5. See 1.
6. Shuler, Frederic, *Flameworking*, 1968, Chilton Book Co.
7. "How Were the Glass Flowers Made?", Botanical Museum Leaflets, Harvard University, Cambridge MA, 1961.
8. *Daum: 100 Years of Glass and Crystal*, Daum et Cie and The Smithsonian Institution, 1978.
9. Grover, Ray and Lee, *Contemporary Art Glass*, Crown Publishers, NY, 1975, pp. 14-19

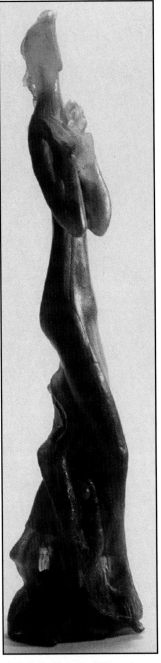

Edris Eckhardt, "Vernal Equinox," 1976. (photo courtesy of the Museum of American Glass, Wheaton Village)

Dan Dailey, "La Dame," pate de verre edition, 1984, Cristalerie Daum, 18" high x 12" wide x 8" deep.
(photo courtesy of the artist)

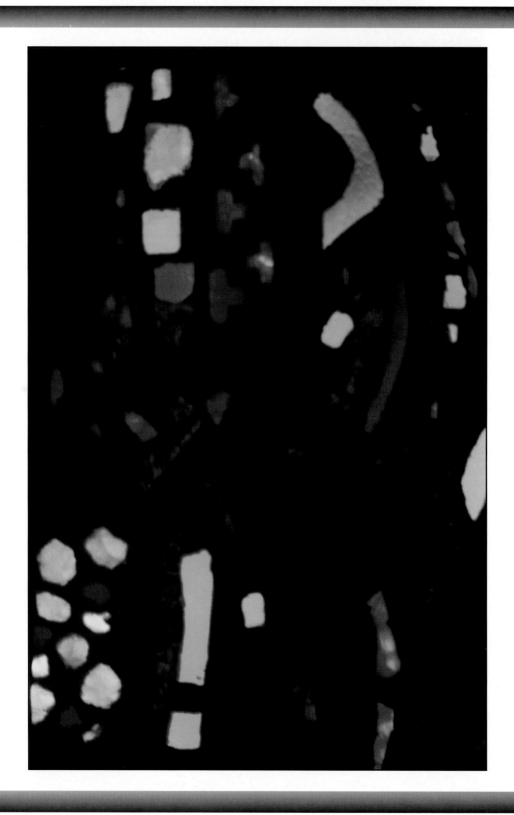

Properties of Glass

An understanding of the physical properties of glass is vital to an artist working with it, both as a material and as a process. The physical procedures involved with many aspects of glass-forming require an active participation; molten glass comes alive in the hands of the artist. The choice of material (type of glass) and the way of working with it are integral elements of the artistic process. To one artist, the thrill of working may be in the nurturing of a glob of molten glass into a beautiful and expressive form; to another, it may be the crackling sound of glass breaking, or the excitement of submitting cold rigid glass to the intense heat of a slumping kiln. The mind, heart, hand and eye of the artist determines the shape and form, which ever way the object is made. Understanding the properties of glass gives the artist the ability to make such choices.

Just what is glass? "Glass is a inorganic product of fusion which has been cooled to a rigid condition without crystallization."[1] So, glass is a rigid liquid. Seems strange when you have a glass filled with water that both the container and the contained are one and the same. The molecules in the glass container are just thicker and appear to be a solid. Remember in sixth grade science class when you learned about gases, liquids and solids? Well, glass is one of those materials that escapes a logical definition.

Glass is produced from inorganic oxides. Silica (or sand) is the most important ingredient. Other oxides present in glass act as modifiers. Soda or potash lowers the melting point, but tends to render the glass too soft. An addition of lime stabilizes and hardens it. Lead softens the glass and adds brilliance. Borax hardens the glass and increases its ability to withstand thermal shock. A broad range of metal oxides give a rainbow of colors as infinite as the spectrum.

Silica occurs in a variety of crystalline forms; quartz, tridymite, cristobalite, flint, agate and opal. Next to oxygen, silicon is the most abundant element found in nature. The most common type of silica used for glassmaking comes from quartz in the form of sand. Much of the sand used today is mined from underground deposits or quarried from sandstone formations. The finest deposits contain as much as 99% pure silica; however, they also contain iron oxides. These iron oxides cause the glass to have a green or yellow color.

Crushed flint, as a form of silica, was first used in England in the late 17th century by George Ravenscroft. Natural flint is found in pebble form along the coasts of England and France. The glass known as "crystal" was exceptionally brilliant and highly light refractive. Because flint was very hard and difficult to crush, sand and lead were substituted. However, the term "flint glass" still applies today to lead crystal.

Soda or **soda ash** (sodium carbonate) is obtained from salt-water lake brines, as well as a synthetic process; it acts as a flux to lower the melting point of pure silica (3,000F). It produces a glass that is soft and lacks strength. Limestone is added to the mixture as a stabilizer and to increase strength. It could also include barium and feldspar. This soda-lime-silica combination is the most common type of glass produced today. It is found in bottles, containers, most window glass, art glass and glass art. It is similar in composition to the very earliest known glasses.

Potash (potassium carbonate) is obtained from natural mined potassium salts; like soda, it acts as a flux to lower the melting point of silica. Glasses made from a potash mixture are harder than the soda-lime glasses; however, the viscosity is higher, and they are more difficult to work. The addition of lead oxide lowers the viscosity and extends the working range. Because potash and lead are expensive ingredients, their use is limited to the best quality art glass and optical glass. Lead glasses may contain varying amounts of lead oxide. Very high lead content glasses are ideal for cast sculpture, because they have a low melting temperature and a high coefficient of expansion, plus they have excellent refractive qualities and are ideal for cutting and engraving.

Borax (boric acid), a la Twenty Mule Team, is a mineral and prepared chemical compound made from tincal. Borax shares with silica the ability to form a glassy compound when fused. It also acts as a fluxing agent; however, its greatest advantage when added to a glass formula is a low coefficient of expansion. This allows the glass to resist thermal shock. It is a hard glass and can resist chemical attack. Borosilicate glasses, as they are known, melt at a higher temperature and are more difficult to fabricate. They are primarily used for laboratory glassware and household cookware (Pyrex, for example, is a Corning Glass Co., trademark). Borosilicate glass is manufactured into rods and tubes, of a seemingly infinite range of sizes. For many years, lampworkers have reshaped these into scientific apparatus and sometimes even swans and unicorns. This glass does have definite advantages when working with heavy forms. Its low coefficient of expansion makes it ideal for forming large thick pieces of glass.

The lost wax casting experiments conducted by Frederick Carder in the 1930s were done exclusively with PYREX cullet. He claims it was recycled from his own kitchen.

Translucent or **opaque glasses** are called opals. Nonmetal crystalline particles having a different index of refraction are introduced either as a fluoride or a phosphate. These cause small particles to crystallize as the glass is cooled. The effect so created scatters light within the body of the glass and diffuses the transmitted light.

There are other categories of specialty glasses such as **aluminosilicates** and **fused silicas**. Most of these are used in the space industry and for high temperature cookware. One interesting category is **optical glasses**. These glasses are based on rare earth oxides and contain little or no silica. Lanthanum and thorium, when fused, make ideal optical glasses. Prisms made from them have the ability to equally bend light of all colors, thus they make great camera lenses. Another glass containing neodymium and praseodymium is known as didymium. It transmits all colors except yellow, making it ideal for safety glasses and theatrical spotlights. Photo-sensitive and photochromic glasses contain

Changing the Colors of Glass

When glass is left uncolored, or in a natural state, its color is a pale green. Additional colors can be created by using small amounts of metallic oxides. Nickel and manganese produce purple; cobalt and copper make blues, chromium and iron both make green, uranium produces a greenish yellow and cadmium can make a yellow or orange. Both cadmium and selenium make reds and so can copper. Silver produces a wide range of yellows, and gold can make reds that range from pale pink to a rich ruby red. The rare earth neodymium oxide is magic—in tungsten light it appears to be light purple, in fluorescent light it turns to an icy blue.

Any iron compounds present in the sand, even in small amounts, introduces a green tint to the glass. To neutralize this effect, it is necessary to add other oxidizing agents to the glass. Arsenic (arsenious oxide), potassium nitrate or sodium nitrate all release oxygen into molten glass and minimize the coloring effect of the iron oxide and the glass appears clear. Another way to de-colorize is by adding a neutralizing metallic oxide to the glass. Manganese or cobalt in very dilute amounts will alter the natural green color so that the glass appears to be clear.

Double-rolled hand-cast sheet glass. (photo courtesy of Bullseye Glass Co.)

Single-rolled hand-cast fracture-streamer glass. (photo courtesy of Bullseye Glass Co.)

Sheet glass is crushed into frit, screened and jarred in four grain sizes. (photo courtesy of Bullseye Glass Co., photo by Russell Johnson)

ultraviolet light-sensitive metals, gold, silver or copper. The selective development of color can be controlled by placing a mask or photographic film in contact with the glass. When exposed to ultraviolet radiation, then heated, the glass changes from clear to opal, reproducing the pattern on the glass. The image developed is permanent and will not fade as would a similar image in photochromic glass. Photochromic glasses simply darken when exposed to ultraviolet radiation. The most familiar of these glasses are photo-gray sunglasses.

Bullseye: Bullseye Glass Co. in Portland, Oregon, was founded by glass artists to supply the growing stained glass industry. Each sheet of glass is hand cast. The molten glass is ladled from a tank onto a casting table, then fed through a trough to a stationary cast iron rolling table. Multi-colored glasses are mixed by hand on the casting table before it is rolled out. Because the owners of Bullseye were glass artists themselves, they were aware of the growing interest in casting and fusing. They went to great lengths to adjust their formulas to provide a suitable glass for artists to use.

Window glass is a material used today by many artists in an ever expanding exploration of artistic directions. The Romans used glass for glazing windows; fragments of broken window panes were found when the city of Pompeii was dug from its blanket of lava. Until the 20th century, window glass was either blown into a large disc called a rondel, or a long cylinder was blown first then slumped to flatten. Thick plate glass was cast. Slabs were formed by ladling glass onto large iron casting tables, then ground and polished by hand. Today, most window glass is made by the float glass process. An endless ribbon of molten glass floats across the surface of a bath of molten tin. The temperature of the tin is gradually decreased as the glass moves across the surface until it is rigid enough to enter the annealing lehr. The surfaces of float glass are very flat and parallel.

Flat or **stained glass** was made by rolling. Originally, the molten glass was ladled onto an iron table and rolled out into a flat sheet by hand with a heavy iron roller. Machines now replace hand techniques (with some exceptions). There are a few small hand factories that approach the creation of their glass as an art form.

Antique glass refers to the hand-blown cylinders that are opened and flattened by a slumping process.

Blenko: Blenko Glass Co., in Milton, West Virginia, makes flat glass by blowing large cylinders and slumping them flat. They also cast large thick slabs of glass called dalle de verre. There is an entire vocabulary related to the manufacture of colored flat glass.

Cathedral glass refers to clear-colored sheet glass, hand-rolled or machine-made.

Flash glass can be antique or machine-made. It has a very thin coating of intense colored-glass over a clear or opaque base.

Opalescent glass made opaque

Hand-blowing large cylinder for slumping into flat glass, Blenko Glass Co. (photo by the author)

Hand-cast slabs of glass, Blenko Glass Co. (photo by the author)

with additions of phosphates or fluorides to the batch when it is melted. It can be hand-rolled or machine-made.

Semi-antique glass is blown with the aid of an air compressor. The cylinders are much larger.

Streakies made when opal glass and transparent glass are mixed and rolled into a pattern. These can be hand-rolled or machine-made.

Iridescents are made by fuming vapors of tin chloride, titanium chloride or silver nitrate while the glass is hot. Most often found on opalescent glasses.

Dichroic glasses: Dichroic comes from the Greek word for "two-color." A coating is applied to the surface of glass in a vacuum chamber by evaporation of inorganic materials which form many thin layers on the glass. Light reflects one color and transmits a different one.

Reference

1. The American Society for Testing and Materials. Glass, J.R. Hutchins III and R.V. Harrington, Corning Glass Works, reprinted from Kirk-Othmer: *Encyclopedia of Chemical Technology*, 2nd Edition Volume 10, 1966, John Wiley & Sons, 1966, p. 534

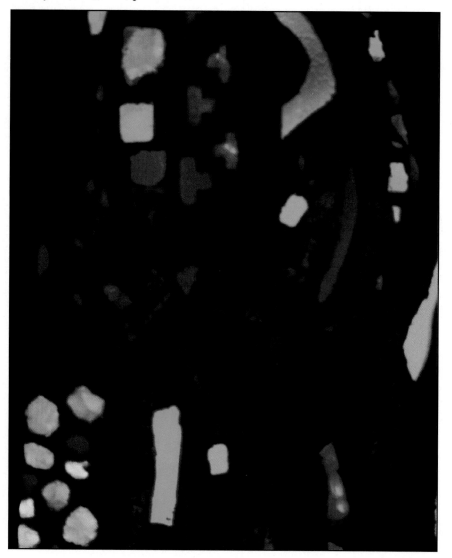

Close-up of window using dalle de verre (thick slabs), Blenko Glass Co. (photo by the author)

Section 3

Glassforming with a Furnace

Glassblowing

The traditional method of hand blowing glass has changed very little over the centuries. The following description written in 1556 by Agricola would be appropriate today in a small glass studio.

"He takes up just as much as he needs to complete the article he wishes to make; then he presses it against the lip of marble and kneads it round and round until it consolidates. When he blows through the pipe he blows as he would if inflating a bubble: he blows into the blowpipe as often as it is necessary, removing it from his mouth to re-fill his cheeks, so that his breath does not draw the flame into his mouth. Then, twisting the lifted blow-pipe round his head in a circle, he makes a long glass, or moulds the same in a hollow copper mould, turning it round and round, then warming it again, blowing and pressing it, he widens it into the shape of a cup or vessel, or of any other object he has in mind. Then he again presses this against the marble to flatten the bottom, which he moulds in the interior with his other blowpipe. Afterward he cuts out the lip with shears, and, if necessary adds feet and handles."[2]

This description, with some changes in terms and more sophisticated tools, is still how glass is blown. The directions seem rather simple, the complexities lie in the skill of the craftsman. All glass was hand-blown in small glass houses by teams of skilled artisans until early in the 20th century. Most of the glass produced in these shops was functional and commercial; however, during breaks and after hours many of the craftsmen would allow their creativity free reign. Some marvelous objects were created as a result. The advent of large production machines early in the 20th century removed the artisan from the glass, especially in America, as a result, creative glassblowing became a lost art for a time.

Maurice Marinot

A forerunner of the contemporary studio glass movement was the French Fauvist painter Maurice Marinot. In 1911, Marinot visited a small glass works run by his friends the Viard brothers. He was stunned by the beauty of the colored glass and expressed a desire to use the material. With the Viard Brothers' help, he began to design vessels that he decorated with paints and enamels. He soon began to work directly with the glass himself, and the surface decoration became less important than the mass of the glass object. He gave up painting; by 1925,

Maurice Marinot, bottle with stopper, 1927, 5-1/2" high x 3-3/4" wide x 2-7/8" diameter. (photo courtesy of The Corning Museum of Glass)

he had gained national recognition for his glass objects. In a catalog preface for an exhibition in New York in 1932, his glass was compared to the paintings of Matisse and the sculptures of Rodin, who was also attracted to glass, and had one of his masks cast in *pate de verre* in 1911. The mask is in the Rodin Museum in Paris.

The Family Tree

Harvey Littleton, the father of the studio movement in the United States, was directly influenced by the work of Marinot. Professor Littleton was born in Corning, New York, and spent several summers working for the Corning Glassworks. Although his early career was spent teaching and working as a potter at the Toledo Art Museum and the University of Wisconsin, he had a vision of working with glass as a medium for art. The American Craft Council and the Toledo Art Museum helped to realize this dream by sponsoring two seminars in the summer of 1962.

Dominick Labino, then director of research for Johns Manville, became involved in the project; they were able to successfully melt and blow glass that summer on the museum grounds. The following September, the first university glass program was introduced by Professor Littleton on the graduate level at the University of Wisconsin. From these courageous beginnings the "Family Tree" of glassblowing has grown to include glass facilities in colleges and universities worldwide. In the United States alone, there are thousands of small studios where artists are using glass in a creative way.

Harvey K. Littleton, blowing glass in his studio, Spruce Pine, NC. (photo by the author)

Harvey K. Littleton, blowing glass in his studio, Spruce Pine, NC. (photo by the author)

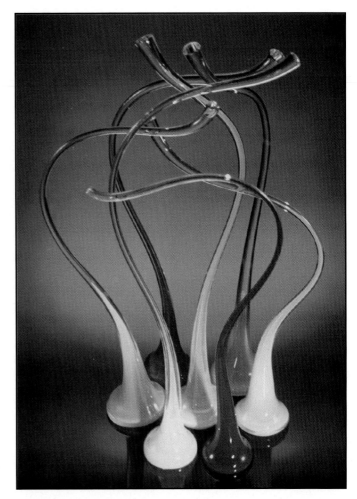

Harvey K. Littleton, "Yellow, Orange and Red Implied Movement," 1987, glass, 38.5" high x 44" wide x 10" deep. (photo courtesy of the Littleton Co., Inc.)

Cultural Ambassador

Soon after, there was an explosion of creative energy. The enthusiasm of the artist-turned-glassblower led to experimenting and developing the skills needed to create art made from glass. Marvin Lipofsky was one of Harvey Littleton's first graduate students. He saw immediately the potential for creating sculptural forms in glass. His direction was to explore all possible forms glass can assume at the end of a blowpipe, often incorporating intense color and texture. The forms were sometimes cut apart or fractured, often reassembled to create strong sculptural statements. His greatest contribution to the advancement of the material glass, used as an art form, has been through travel and teaching. He has traveled all over the world, working in studios and factories with some of the world's most renowned artists and craftsmen. Much of Lipof-

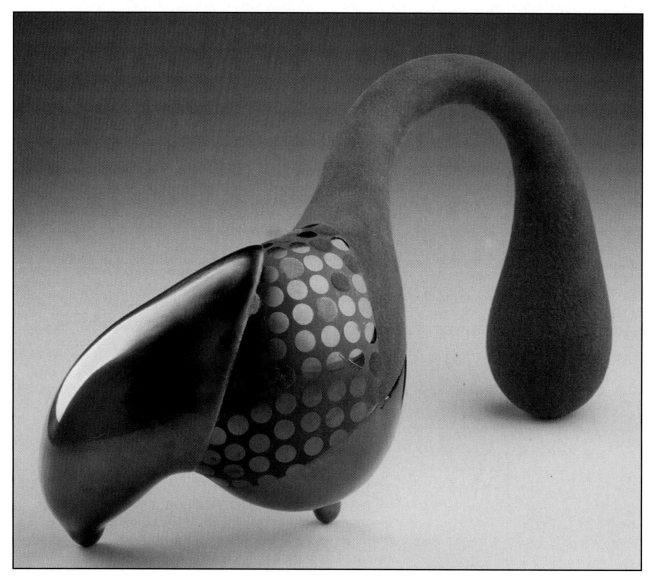

Marvin Lipofsky, "California Loop Series," 1970, glass and mixed media, 10" high x 18" wide. (photo courtesy of the artist, photo by M. Lee Fatherree)

sky's work has been executed this way; each series reflects the cultural traditions and technical experience gained through working in other cultures. His enthusiasm opened other more traditional cultures to the creative potentials of glass as a fine art form.

Marvin Lipofsky, "Violetta Series," 1992-96 #16, Stronie Sloskie, Poland, Crystal Glass Factory "Violetta" Stronie Slaskie Poland with help from glass master Skiba. (photo courtesy of the artist, photo by M. Lee Fatherree)

31

Team Sport

Another early student of Littleton's was Dale Chihuly, the one glass artist's name everyone knows. His greatest contribution was the founding of The Pilchuck School near Seattle, Washington. That in turn helped to make Seattle the glass art capitol of the United States and also helped to create an awareness of glass as an art form accessible to all. His other great contribution was the importance of artists working together as a team in the old glass factory traditions. Glassblowing really is a team sport. Although you can blow glass on your own, very few artists do. To create ambitious pieces, most artists work in pairs or teams.

After a severe car accident many years ago, Chihuly gathered a team of glass artists together to execute his ideas–an idea that goes back to the original Venetian factory concept of a master gaffer and a team of assistants. This teamwork is wonderful to watch. It's like watching a ballet where every move is critical and dependent on the

Dale Chihuly drawing, Creative Glass Center of America, Glass Lovers Weekend, 1991. (photo courtesy of CGCA, Wheaton Village, NJ)

Dale Chihuly instructing team, Creative Glass Center of America, Glass Lovers Weekend, 1991. (photo courtesy of CGCA, Wheaton Village, NJ)

Dale Chihuly's team, Lino Tagliapietra, chief gaffer, Creative Glass Center of America, Glass Lovers Weekend, 1991. (photo courtesy of CGCA, Wheaton Village, NJ)

movement before and the one just after. It's a synchronized choreography ending with an object whose presence exists as a separate entity.

Dale Chihuly, Venetian, 1991, 18" high x 12" wide x 12" diameter, blown at Creative Glass Center of America, Glass Lovers Weekend, 1991. (photo courtesy of the Museum of American Glass, Wheaton Village, NJ)

This book is about learning to use glass as a material; however, the subject of glass-blowing is a hands-on process and very difficult to step-by-step guide a novice through, even blowing a first bubble. The text would be a book unto itself, as it would have to include building a glass furnace, melting the glass and building all of the other related equipment. It certainly is possible. I strongly recommend anyone interested in learning to blow glass take classes first. There are many possibilities; many colleges and universities have glass departments, and summer schools such as Pilchuck and Penland in North Carolina offer classes in a variety of forming processes. The Studio of the Corning Museum School in Corning, New York, and Urban Glass in Brooklyn have intensive workshops, plus a variety of smaller studios around the country referred to as "Studio Access" are teaching classes and renting time in the hot shop.

Casting with Hot Glass

Early references to how glass was actually cast into a mold are vague. Some examples found in antiquities collections appear to have been cast using the lost wax process, a bronze casting technique well known to the ancient Syrians and Egyptians. Early references to glass called it a metal. Was the glass ladled from a pot or furnace into a mold? Some artifacts from the Roman period indicate the use of glass powders pressed into a mold and fired in an oven of sorts. The *pate de verre* method of casting glass appears to be the most often employed technique throughout history.

A growing number of artists are casting from the tank of molten glass directly into molds. Casting with hot glass requires a glass furnace, as well as the knowledge and skill to handle the molten material. Size can present a problem, as the glass has to be ladled from a tank into a mold. This is a difficult process, because it involves handling heavy ladles made even heavier by the weight of extremely hot glass.

Handling large amounts of glass from a tank requires strength, and the entire operation must be accomplished quickly. If the glass in the mold cools too rapidly or is delayed entering the annealing oven, it is subject to stress and cracking. If the piece is quite large, the glass should be ladled into the mold while the mold is in the annealing oven. It's not so easy to move around very large and hot molds.

One way to overcome the issue of size is to incorporate the mold and the annealing oven as one unit in relation to the furnace. The glass is dropped or channeled into the mold while it is in the oven. When the mold is filled, the glass and mold are then subject to the appropriate annealing cycle.

Gene Koss, "River-Dam-Run-Gizmo Contraption," *fabricated by Neil Harshfield, 1997, cast glass, steel, 70" high x 26" wide x 26" deep. (photo courtesy of the artist)*

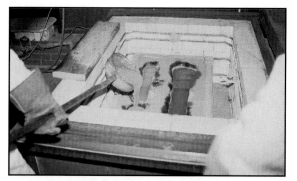

Mark Abildgaard, casting into sand mold in annealer. (photo courtesy of the Creative Glass Center of America)

Molds for Casting Hot Glass

Metal molds. Glass has been cast into metal molds for hundreds of years. As long as the glass can fall out of the mold when turned upside down, the mold can be used over again. Slabs and *dalles de verre* are cast hot in steel frames that are clamped together. Any type metal can be used except aluminum and lead, as their melting points are very low. Molds must be preheated, but kept cooler than the molten glass, because hot glass will permanently stick to hot metal.

Gene Koss has been casting directly into metal "gizmos," as he calls them. They are metal forms that are both sculpture and mold.

Graphite molds. Graphite is becoming a popular material for making molds for hot casting, as it withstands thermal-shock and can be easily machined into patterns with a dremel tool. Shape it outdoors and wear a mask, as it is quite messy. It can be worth the trouble though; glass will not stick to graphite when it gets too hot and a mold can be used over many times. It is important to preheat any mold for hot casting as a cold mold will cause the glass to bubble and blister.

Refractory molds. Plaster/silica molds can be used to cast into with molten glass. For large castings, a back-up coat of a dense refractory or a ceramic shell mold is recommended. Mold Mix Six from Zircar also works well. The refractory mold should be preheated to about 1400F prior to casting.

Sandcasting: Sandcasting is a process of ladling hot glass into impressions made by pressing a positive model into a bed of sand. Mark Abildgaard built his molds directly in the oven to avoid handling such large amounts of hot glass for annealing.

Mark Abildgaard, "Glass Totems," glass cast in sand molds, 1985, 36" high x 10" wide x 6" deep.

Bertil Vallien is the granddaddy of all sand casters. In Sweden, where he lives and works for Kosta Boda Glass Company, he began casting glass into sand molds in the early 1970s. Some of his sand-cast boat forms are very large and could only be made with factory-size equipment. In 1997, he was invited to Bullseye Glass Company to execute some of his large pieces.

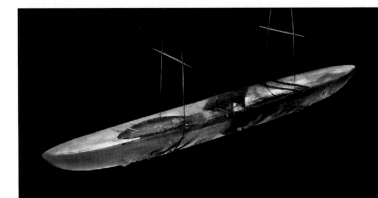

Bertil Vallien, "Pendulum," 1987. (photo courtesy of Heller Gallery, by Anders Qwarnstrom)

Bertil Vallien prepares a sand mold at the Bullseye factory, March 1997. (photo courtesy of the Bullseye Glass Co., photo by Russell Johnson)

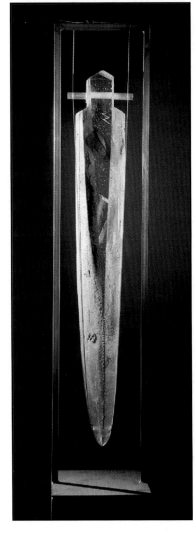

Pre-formed blown and kiln-worked inclusions are added to the casting during the pour. (photo courtesy of the Bullseye Glass Co., photo by Russell Johnson)

Left and above: Bertil Vallien, "Celestial Voyager," 55" high x 12" wide x 12" deep. (photo courtesy of Heller Gallery, by Anders Qwarnstrom)

Doug Ohm manipulates the hot glass in the mold. This is a difficult operation as the timing must be perfect to move the glass while still hot enough and get it into the annealing oven before it cools too much.

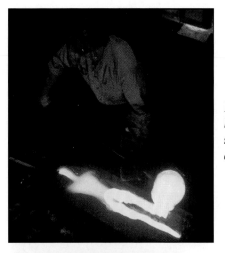

Douglas Ohm, ladling glass into sand mold. (photo courtesy of the artist)

Douglas Ohm, manipulating glass in the sand mold. (photo courtesy of the artist)

Douglas Ohm, manipulating glass in the sand mold and keeping the casting hot with a torch. (photo courtesy of the artist)

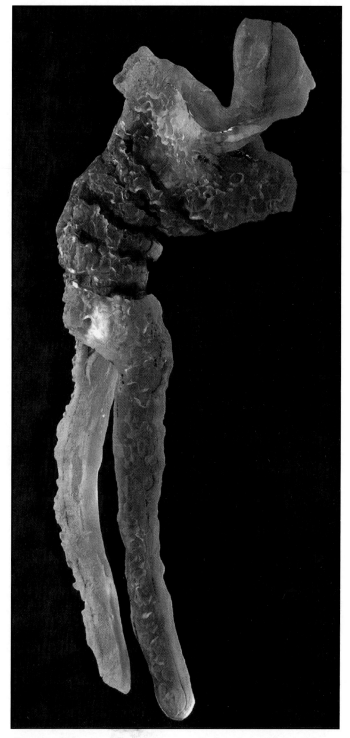

Douglas Ohm, untitled figure, manipulated cast glass with copper inclusions, 1995, 36" high x 8" wide x 4" deep. (photo courtesy of the artist)

Making a Sand Mold

1. To begin, build a box 4" deeper than the deepest impression and fill with sand.
2. To the dry sand, add 10%-15% bentonite and enough water to moisten the mixture. Just enough so the sand sticks together when you gather a fist full.
3. Any object without serious undercuts can be used to make an impression in the sand. Wood, metal, cast plaster, even wet clay can be used. It helps to install a handle to facilitate removal from the sand bed.
4. After the imprint is complete and any loose sand is removed, a layer of carbon is added. This can be done with spray graphite or by carbonizing with the gas line from an acetylene torch. Acetylene is a dirty burning fuel, it makes lots of black sooty carbon which is good for molds but not the environment. Use good ventilation.

(photo courtesy of the artist)

(photo courtesy of the artist)

5. At this time, compatible glass powders could be added. After the first few gathers or pours, powders can be added again, as well as preheated inclusions made from compatible glass.

6. If the casting has a large surface exposed to uneven cooling, it helps to have a propane torch handy to keep everything at an even temperature. If bubbles occur, the sand is too moist. Heating them with a torch sometimes brings them to the surface where they can be popped.

7. When the glass is rigid enough to remove from the sand, it is placed in an oven and annealed.

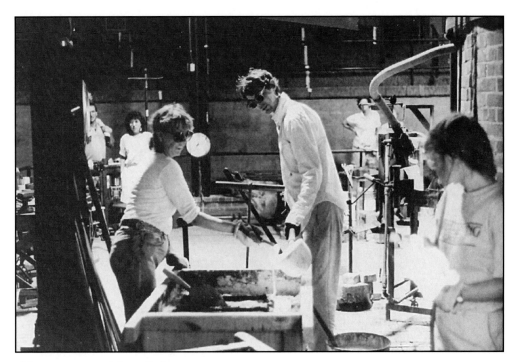

(photo courtesy of the artist)

Gasbond Sand Mix[1]

This process is a method for making rigid sand molds from a sodium silicate binder which is chemically bonded with CO_2 gas. CO_2 gas is blown into the mixture at intervals to set the sand. The mold is used like regular sand molds for casting; however, its green strength is much stronger for intricate detail or for ladling large amounts of glass.

1. Dry sand and gasbond binder are mixed together in a separate container in amounts of from 2% to 5% binder. Place an object without undercuts in a box, allowing several inches all around it. Fill the box with the sand and gasbond binder mixture over the object and pack it down hard.
2. Make a nozzle from a 1/4″ diameter copper tube about 12″ long with 1/8″ holes drilled at 1/2″ intervals. This is attached to the hose from the CO_2 tank.
3. Set the tank gauge at 40 PSI. Insert the tube in the sand mix and gas for 20 to 30 seconds at frequent intervals to set the sand. The gas must permeate through all of the sand mix.
4. When properly gassed, the mold will be rigid. The positive model is carefully removed and a coating of carbon or graphite is added before casting.
5. To cast, follow directions for sand casting.

References

1. For further information, see *Glass Notes* by Henry Halem in "Bibliography" or United Erie, Inc., under "Supply Source."
2. *De Re Metalica*, Agricola, Dover Publishing.

Lampworking

Like the history of so many other glassmaking techniques, the early history of lampworking is constantly being rewritten, and established dates are being pushed farther back in time. Current research is coming up with evidence of the use of a direct flame to shape glass as early as the New Kingdom, Egypt. To date, nothing has been published to document the evidence; however, it won't be long before a new history of flameworking will be written.

The term lampworking goes back to the 17th century when the flame of a gas lamp was used to melt small globules of glass. These small bits of glass were then ground and polished for use as microscope lenses. The advantage of using a torch or small flame to remelt and form glass is primarily one of scale. The intense heat of a glass furnace makes it almost impossible to work up close on very small objects. In addition to microscope lenses, other objects made by early lampworkers were hollow beads, lenses for lamps and cameras, scientific apparatus for laboratories and even Edison's first light bulb.

The cane (rods) and tubes used by lampworkers are formed hot from a tank of molten glass. To form a cane by hand, the glass is gathered several times onto a punteil (a 5-foot stainless steel rod) and marvered (rolled on a steel table called a marver) into a conical shape. A second ponteil is attached to the cone by an assistant. The assistant then walks backward, pulling and stretching the glass into a long rod. The thickness of the rod can be determined by the temperature of the glass, the rate of speed it's pulled and the amount of glass on the ponteil. Glass can be pulled into very thin straws as fine as fibers or into rods as thick as several inches. Tubes are formed similarly; however, a blowpipe is used to blow a bubble into the first gather. Then successive gathers are added to make the walls thicker. The bubble is blown out enough so that it won't collapse. A ponteil is attached by an assistant and pulled out to form a hollow tube.

Pyrex

Pyrex (this trademark name has become synonymous with all like products) or borosilicate and some soda/lime or soft glass rods and tubes are now manufactured by machines in large factories. The molten glass is pulled into continuous rods or tubes from a furnace. These long rods or tubes travel across a lehr about 30-feet long with gas jets slowly cooling them to room temperature. At the end of the lehr they are cut into 4-feet lengths and packed into boxes. The production of this type of glass is primarily directed toward scientific applications. A large percentage of scientific apparatus is still hand-formed in the laboratory from manufactured tubes and rods. How many of us have had the experience of trying to melt glass from a Bunsen burner in high school chemistry class?

The basic equipment used by the lampworker is relatively simple: a torch, fuel (propane or natural gas), oxygen, some shaping tools and an annealing oven. The rods or tubes are formed into innumerable shapes by working the glass directly in the flame of the torch. Solid, as well as hollow-blown forms, can be created with flame-working techniques. Although the equipment required may be simple, the technical skill required of the craftsman is demanding.

Except for the artistic techniques developed by the Bohemian lampworkers Leopold Blaschka and his son Rudolph to create

Scientific tubing cullet pile.

Ginny Ruffner, "Conceptual Narratives Series/The Content is the Decoration," 1997, glass and mixed media, 23" high x 23" wide x 25" deep. (photo courtesy of the artist)

realistic botanical and zoological models as well as delicate flowers, the first few decades of the 20th century saw very few artists using the torch as a tool for making art.

The scientific use of lampworked glass goes back to the early 18th century when the laboratory was leaving the mysticism of alchemy and entering the era of science. Even today, laboratory use requires one-of-a-kind shape, size and function of glass apparatus. Many research facilities employ full-time scientific lampworkers to execute this highly-specialized equipment. Ginny Ruffner uses this scientific laboratory glass to make her whimsical, autobiographical works of art. She bends, stretches and shapes rods and tubes of borosilicate glass into these fantasy shapes, then sandblasts and paints them, often combining found objects.

Interest Grows

After the Depression in the United States, interest in all types of glass objects grew. Scientific lampworkers began to make animals, novelties and hollow-blown ware from borosilicate glass on their breaks, just as the furnace glass-blowers had done for centuries.

Milon Townsend uses the flame to sculpt solid figures in borosilicate glass and assembles them in a suggestive scenario. His figures reflect his interest in movement and dance. Like many other artists today, he is combining other types of forming processes in his work.

Milon Townsend, "Descent," 1997, clear glass with gold diachroic wrap, assembled with plate glass, 26" high. (photo courtesy of the artist)

Milon Townsend, "Shock wave," 1997, colored figure with bent plate glass, 10" high x 6" wide x 6" deep. (photo courtesy of the artist)

The advantage of using a torch to form glass is the ability to work up close and very small. Early paperweight makers found it difficult to make small detailed inclusions from the end of a 5-foot long ponteil. Millifiore and delicate flowers inside the mid-19th century French paperweights were lampworked first, then picked up with hot glass and finished at the gaffer's bench. During the 1939 World's Fair, a traveling troupe of German lampworkers caught the attention of Charles Kaziun, a scientific lampworker for the University of Pennsylvania. Kaziun was interested in paperweights and made friends with many of the South Jersey tank glass makers including Emil Larson, famous for the Millville Rose weight. Kaziun was encouraged to experiment; by the mid 1940s, he was the first to make completely lampworked paperweights.

Tiny Works of Art

Paul Stankard relocated to South Jersey many years ago and was influenced by Kaziun's paperweights. Stankard continued the lampworked paperweight tradition developing finer and more delicate imagery in his work. His love of nature and his passion for recreating beauty combined to make his paperweights highly collectable. Paralleling his development as a lampworker was his interest in glass as art. He began collecting the work of other artists and took great interest in learning more about other techniques in glass, as well as painting and sculpture. During the course of his career, he created an awareness of the importance of glass as an art form which, in turn, influenced his own perception of his format–the paperweight. The result has been a marriage of fine art and consummate craftsmanship, resulting in the acceptance of Paul Stankard's renderings in glass as an excellent example of fine art.

Paul J. Stankard, "Pollinating Mosaic," 1997, 7-1/2" x 16-3/4" wide x 2-1/4" deep. (photo courtesy of the artist, photo by James Amos)

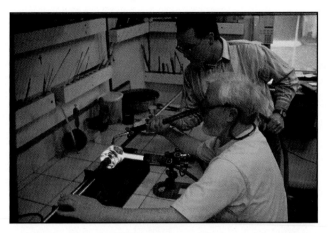

Paul J. Stankard at the torch.

Close-up of Paul J. Stankard at the torch. (photo courtesy the artist, photo by James Amos)

Paul J. Stankard, "Close-up of Coronets with Root Spirits and Honeybee Botanical," 1996, 5-1/2" high. (photo courtesy of the artist, photo by John Taylor)

Paul J. Stankard, "Coronet Botanical Cube," 1995, 5-1/4" h. (photo courtesy the artist, photo by John Taylor)

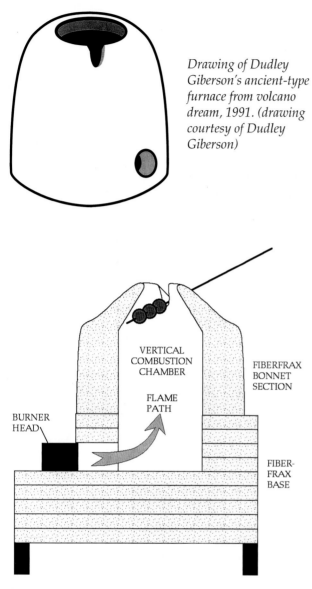

Drawing of Dudley Giberson's ancient-type furnace from volcano dream, 1991. (drawing courtesy of Dudley Giberson)

VERTICAL COMBUSTION CHAMBER

FLAME PATH

FIBERFRAX BONNET SECTION

BURNER HEAD

FIBER-FRAX BASE

Drawing of Dudley Giberson's "Generation 3 Bead-maker," the one he and his partner Carolyn Rordam use now. (drawing courtesy Dudley Giberson)

Massi beadmaker, Kitengela Glass, Nairobi, Kenya. (photo by the author)

Glass Beads

Five-thousand years ago, someone made beads from glass. It's very likely that beads were the first objects ever produced from glass. The fact that glass beads are still being made worldwide, mostly by hand, is pretty amazing. The high-tech society we live in has given us modern sophisticated tools and techniques speeding up production and producing a uniform quality to both execution and design of glass beads.

Some artists are looking back to ancient ways, both for aesthetic inspiration and intellectual curiosity. One artist, Dudley Giberson, has been making drawn beads for 20 years based on his idea of how the ancients made them long before the invention of the blow pipe. In 1991, an important dream came to Dudley: "I was sitting before a volcano shape emitting intense heat from its interior, upon which a mandrel full of glass beads was roasting and as the beads got hotter, they rounded into balls–perfect glass beads." He awoke with great excitement and went to his studio. Within a few minutes he put together a "hot volcano." This breakthrough in duplicating ancient furnace design led

Carolyn Rordam making a bead in the furnace. (photos courtesy Dudley Giberson)

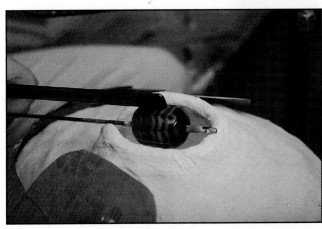
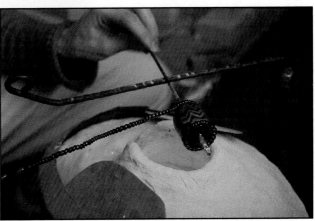

Carolyn Rordam making a bead in the furnace.

him to further research and fabricate sand core vessels and to perfect the vertical furnace design that he uses to make beads with his partner Carolyn Rordam.

Beadmaking, especially flameworked bead making, has become very popular these days. Compared to most glassmaking techniques it seems rather easy: availability of materials and inexpensive equipment has encouraged many would-be artists to give it a go. The seductiveness of the tiny works of art and the deceptive level of skill required to execute them is often frustrating to a beginner. Unfortunately, like playing a piano, it takes hours and hours of practice.

Glass beads. (photo courtesy of Dudley Giberson/Carolyn Rordam, photo by Charley Freiberg)

Glass beads. (photo courtesy of Dudley Giberson/Carolyn Rordam, photo by Charley Freiberg)

The author demonstrates beadmaking at Wheaton Village, NJ.
(photo courtesy of the author)

Close-up view of the author demonstrating beadmaking.
(photo courtesy of the author)

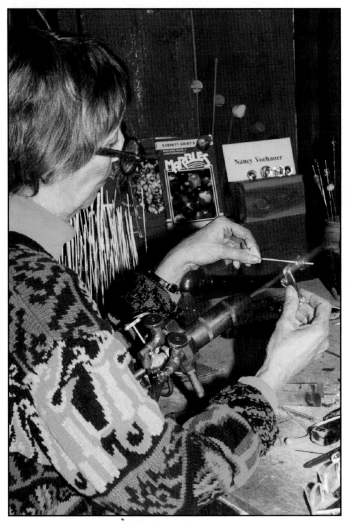

The author demonstrates beadmaking. (photo courtesy of the
author)

How to Make a Bead

Beadmaking is a good technique to start off a lampworking career, especially if you're not into chemistry. The equipment can be relatively inexpensive; a torch can be a simple gas/oxygen burner like the "National" or "Minor" to start off with. The fuel source can be natural gas or propane with oxygen to help the gas burn hot enough to melt the glass. Proper regulators and hoses are needed to connect it all. An exhaust system (at least an open window and a fan) plus a carbon monoxide detector is necessary. Of course, a place to work, plenty of glass and a small annealing oven is very important. Placing a bead in anything other than an annealing oven just won't anneal it. See the "Annealing" section and charts for appropriate schedules.

Step 1.

Setting up a flameworking system
1. Attach the torch firmly to a work table or counter.
2. Install the appropriate regulator on each tank. Check for leaks with soapy water or "Squirty Bubbles Leak Detector."
3. Connect the hoses to the torch, then from the torch to the tank regulators. Red is for gas and green is for oxygen. Check for leaks. If bubbles occur, tighten connections and check again.
4. The gauges on the regulators will tell you how much gas or oxygen is in the tank and the amount of pressure (PSI) released from the tank to the torch. The gas gauge needs to be set at 5 PSI and the oxygen set at 10 PSI.
5. Turn the red gas valve on first (always). Adjust the flame to about a 6" long tail. Slowly turn the green oxygen valve on. A blue point will appear in the red flame. Keep turning the dial until the blue point is about 1/4" to 1/2" long. The hottest part of the flame is about 1-1/2" from the orifice and can be 1800F-2400F, depending on the type of torch.

Step 2.

Get ready to make a tiny work of art
Beads are made by winding glass around a mandrel or wire that has been coated with a release agent. The wire is often 1/16" to 1/8" stainless steel welding stock cut into 12" lengths. These mandrels can be purchased already cut to size from bead-making suppliers. Stainless steel is the best choice, as it is a non-conductor of heat, so the mandrel remains cool while the bead is formed. The release agent is a type of kiln wash with a few added ingredients. There are several versions on the market or one can be made:

    1 pint container
    1/2 cup kaolin (dry)
    1/2 cup alumina hydrate (commercial kiln wash can be used)
    1/4 cup powdered graphite
    1/4 cup zircon flour (try foundry supply companies, but it's okay if you can't find any)
    1 cup water

Mixture should be thick and creamy without any lumps. Or you can use Dudley Giberson's mandrel release: one- or two-parts kaolin to eight- or nine-parts silica, then add water till creamy. Coat by dipping the end of the wire into the jar. Stand erect to dry, overnight if possible. A wood frame with holes drilled in a repeat pattern works, as does a piece of rigid foam or a coffee can filled with sand.

Step 3.

Make a bead

1. The mandrel is slowly heated in the flame with the left hand to remove any moisture from the coating.
2. A glass rod is slowly heated in the flame with the right hand until it softens and forms a round ball. The movements become confusing, similar to those of juggling. One hand is going one way and the other is doing something entirely different.
3. The mandrel in the left hand is held just below the flame and the hot glass rod in the right hand is held above the mandrel directly in the flame. As the glass melts off of the rod, it is wound around the mandrel to build up layers of glass. The bead is built around the hole. Gravity (keeping the glass centered around the wire) and turning the molten glass in the flame, actually make the bead round. Glass, when heated, will naturally form into a round ball. Surface tension causes it to bead-up.
4. The trick to making nicely-shaped round beads is to keep turning the bead after it is out of the direct flame. Most glass remains molten for several minutes. Any interruption of movement during that time can drop a bead off-center and make it crooked.
5. The bead can be decorated at this point or put in the annealing oven.

Beads are a fun way to learn to use a torch. There are several good lampworking books to guide you, as well as workshops and schools teaching lampworking and beadmaking (see "Supply Sources" and "Bibliography" sections).

Section 5

Glassforming with a Kiln

Casting

Several factors are critical to the success of casting glass, either from molten glass or kiln casting–the annealing procedure, the type of mold used and the coefficient of expansion and viscosity of the glass. As cast sculptural forms are three-dimensional, they require very special considerations. It is possible to cast most any size and shape form in glass; however, degrees of difficulty are compounded both by shape and size. Very large cast forms require lengthy annealing cycles and intricate cast forms require complex molds.

Annealing: One of the most critical stages in working with molten glass is the process of slow-cooling or annealing. Hot glass, when cooled, is subject to internal stress. The reason for the annealing procedure is to relieve the internal stress to an acceptable level. There are many theories concerning the principles of proper annealing. Laboratory research and computer technology have taken some of the guesswork out of the time and temperature calculations required to anneal a specific glass object. A few calculations are included in this book. The bottom line is, it's far better to over-anneal an object than to under-anneal it. Sooner or later, the under-annealed object will develop cracks or even break apart, sometimes years later.

Molds: There are many possible materials and techniques for molds suitable for casting glass from either a glass tank or in a kiln. The mold must be strong enough to hold the glass while molten, able to withstand high temperatures and release the glass when cool. For casting hot glass

Lucartha Kohler, "Guardians of the Temple," 1997, installation, glass and mixed media, 6 feet high x 15 feet wide x 4 feet deep; figures lost wax cast in lead crystal with flower pot crucibles, wall figures, 24" high x 4.5" diameter.

from a tank, graphite and metal molds work well. Castable refractories and variations of plaster/silica mold formulas can be used. Moist sand, sodium silicate/CO_2 rigid set sand, resin bond sand and ceramic shell all used in metal casting foundries can also work well for hot glass casting. Plaster/silica (flint) molds work well for kiln-casting small objects. For large objects, a back-up layer of refractory castable with a wire reinforcement makes a stronger mold. Bisque-fired clay, as well as iron and steel, can be used, providing a separator such as kiln wash is used on any surface the glass contacts. There are a number of premixed mold materials on the market made for glass casting and slumping. Most are a variation of the plaster/silica formula with the exception of Zircar's Mold Mix Six which is a thin shell refractory material. All premixed molds are more costly.

Glass: Not all glass is suitable for casting and different types of glass cannot be mixed together in one cast. Glasses are referred to as hard and soft, these terms apply to the softening point of a glass and mean the temperature at which a glass rod bends under its own weight. An example of a hard glass would be a member of the borosilicate family of glass such as "Pyrex." A soft glass would be a member of the soda/lime family of glass such as a glass studio would melt; a lead-bearing glass like your grandmother's Waterford vase would be the softest (with beer bottle and plate glass somewhere in-between). An important property of a glass is its coefficient of expansion (COE), meaning the rate a glass expands and contracts when heated and cooled. Another important property of glass is its viscosity. It is very important when combining different types of glasses together hot that the COE and the viscosity match. When kiln casting, it is even more critical with most glasses that the frit be from the same tank melt. The exception is Bullseye Compatibles: Bullseye takes great care to ensure that its frits and sheet glass are all compatible when they are labeled as such.

Another factor important to selecting a suitable glass for casting is the tendency of a particular glass to devitrify. Devitrification is the formation of crystals in glass. When glass has been held at elevated temperatures (1500F-1800F) for too long, it will leave the liquid state of matter and enter the solid or crystalline state. When crystals form on the surface of glass, they continue to grow. All glass will eventually devitrify if subject to a conducive environment, some more readily than others (depending on their chemical composition).

Evidence of casting techniques exists from ancient times. Until about 250 BC all glass was either core-formed by winding molten threads of glass around a metal rod packed with a core of sand, or it was cast in molds. Very early glassmakers used the technology of metal casting to cast glass and treated it as a "poured stone," incorporating lapidary techniques to cold-work the object. After glassblowing was invented or discovered, cast glass took a backseat for a long time. In the late 19th century, Henry Cros, a Frenchman, became interested in the ancient casting process and began experimenting, using finely ground glass mixed into a paste with a binder. This process he named *pate de verre*.

Eastern Roman pate de verre figurine of Aphrodite, 2nd to 4th century ad, 4-1/4" high. (photo courtesy of Antiquarium, ltd., photo by Justin Kerr)

Henry Cros, plaque with female figure, 1886, pate de verre, 96.3.23, 13.5 cm high x 9.8 cm wide x 1.7 cm thick. (photo courtesy of The Corning Museum of Glass)

A number of artists today are using a version of the *pate de verre* process; however, most are actually casting with frit or even chunks of glass. The term *"pate de verre"* has been used to describe almost all kiln-casting techniques, but there are distinct differences between them. Robin Grebe primarily uses an open-face mold that she paints into with high-fire glass enamels before loading her frit into the mold to fire.

Daniel Clayman works quite large most of the time. He's experimented with many mold materials and developed formulas from some

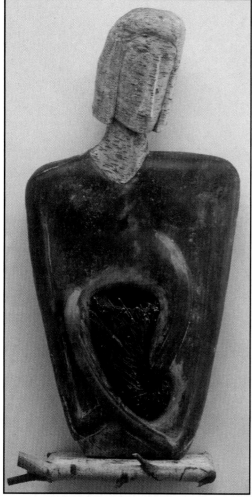

Daniel Clayman, "Reminisci," 1993, glass and copper, 17.5" high, 11" wide x 2" deep. (photo courtesy of the artist)

Robin Grebe, "Sylvan," 1995, glass, wood, birch bark, 32" high x 15" wide x 6-1/2" diameter. (photo courtesy of the artist)

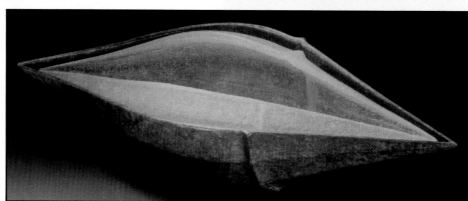

Daniel Clayman, "Hull," 1997, glass and bronze 5.25" high x 16" wide x 5.5" deep. (photo courtesy of the artist)

Mark Abildgaard, "Ancestor Boat," glass, 41" high x 34" wide x 8" deep. (photo courtesy of the artist)

unusual materials. He also uses recycled light bulb glass from a factory for his castings. Mark Abildgaard went from hot casting to kiln casting his totem-like sculptures. Availability of hot glass presents a problem for artists, but the real value of kiln casting is the amount of control an artist has over the process.

Kiln casting is the process of using a kiln, preferably an electric kiln or an annealing oven, as a heat source to melt glass in a refractory or heat-resistant mold. The mold acts like a mini glass tank to hold the glass as it becomes molten. Glass in the form of powder, frit, chunk or rod is placed in the mold cold before it is loaded into the kiln or fed into the mold when the kiln temperature is hot enough to melt the glass. There is a number of terms used to define this process.

Cire perdue (lost wax), ***pate de verre*** (paste of glass), **frit casting** (small kernels of glass called frit), **fuse casting** (chunks, rods or slabs of glass), **drip casting** (a crucible held above the mold with a hole in the bottom to allow the molten glass to flow into a mold) and **slumping** into a mold (a large block of glass placed over or into a mold and melted). *Cire perdue* casting is a mold process. The object to be cast in glass is first modeled or cast in wax from a rubber or plaster mold. This wax model, or positive, is then coated with an investment or refractory mold material. When the mold is dry, the wax is burned or steamed out, leaving a hollow cavity which is an exact negative of the original wax positive. The mold is filled with ground glass then placed in a kiln and fired to a temperature high enough and long enough to melt the glass.

Pate de verre means "paste of glass" in French. The term was used by the early Frenchmen who revived the technique from an even earlier Roman technique. Finely-ground glass is mixed with a gum binder and placed in specific areas of a mold. The advantage of this process is accurate color placement and fine detail. The glass, when fired, has a translucency much like fine porcelain. The reason for the translucent, almost opaque effect, is because the surface of glass particles exposed to high temperatures for extended periods of time have a tendency to devitrify or enter the crystalline state of matter. Imagine a tiny particle of glass with a hazy film all over it bonded together with lots of other hazy particles into a solid mass. That mass then looks almost opaque; also, air gets trapped between the particles of glass to create a luminous effect.

Frit casting or *"chunk de verre"* (as I call the technique) is simply using particles of glass to fill the mold cavity, ranging in size from a seed bead to a marble. The difference between this process and *pate de verre* is the size of the particle of glass or frit. The larger the frit, the clearer the resultant casting. True *pate de verre* has a translucent quality. When you fuse larger bits of glass together, you have less surface-per-bit exposed to higher temperatures, thus less surface devitrification that results in a clearer transparent casting.

Fuse casting means to use large chunks, rods or slabs of glass to fill the mold cavity. This process produces a clear transparent cast. Also, large chunks begin to flow at a lower temperature. It seems that when glass is moving or flowing it does not devitrify as readily. The longer you submit any type of glass to elevated temperatures, the more you increase the chance of surface devitrification. For instance, if you hold your oven at 1650F for several hours after your mold has filled, you can be pretty sure the glass on the exposed surface will have some surface devitrification. It can look hazy or even shriveled like a prune. Once a glass surface has devitrified, it is very difficult to reverse it; however, you can grind it away or sand blast it off and polish the surface if you want it to be shiny.

Drip casting refers to a process of placing a crucible with a hole in the bottom set over a mold in a kiln. (A terra-cotta flower pot placed over the refractory mold is an inexpensive method a number of artists have used.) The pot is filled with glass, then heated to casting temperature. The glass when molten, begins to drip into the mold and, over time, fills the mold cavity. This process works best for deep molds. It also produces the clearest casting as the glass is constantly flowing into the mold.

Slump casting is a process of melting a precast block or chunk of similar size and shape into a mold. This method also produces very clear castings, provided the block or chunk is clear and transparent to begin with.

View of kiln with flower pot crucibles.

Lucartha Kohler, "Artifact Torso," 24" high x 12" wide, cast glass. (photo courtesy of the artist)

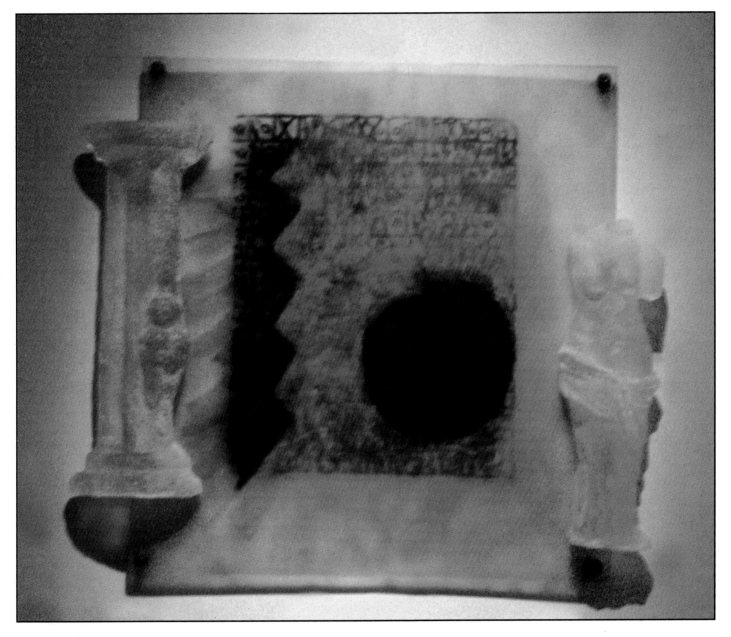

Lucartha Kohler, "Times Transparent Veil," 24" high x 30" wide, cast glass, silk-screen print. (photo courtesy of the artist)

Frit Casting

Another version of kiln casting is called "frit casting." Frit casting is a variation of *pate de verre* and is sometimes mistakenly referred to as such. The primary difference is the size of the frit or chunk of glass you place in the mold cavity and the appearance of the finished object. The larger the chunk of glass, the clearer and more transparent the object.

The size of the frit can vary from Bullseye #3 frit, which is pea size, to large chunks of cullet, even scraps of sheet glass and bits of broken blown-ware are castable as long as they are compatible.

The mold processes are the same. The open-face process covered under *pate de verre* is the easiest. Any mold technique and any refractory material can be used as an investment. If your positive model is large or deep, you will need to build a reservoir to hold the excess glass necessary to fill the mold with molten glass. By placing large chunks in the mold, you allow for more air space around each chunk and increase the volume of glass needed to fill the mold. This reservoir acts like a feeder cup. As the glass melts, it flows down into the mold cavity from the reservoir.

Preparing the glass for frit casting is a bit easier. If you bought Bullseye, all you have to do is fill the mold directly from the canister it came in. Most likely you will want to wash whatever else you are using and perhaps break very large chunks into more manageable ones. Frit casting works best for high-temperature charging as large chunks will explode in the kiln from thermal shock.

Lucartha Kohler, "Hypnos and the Dreamer," 12" high x 16" wide x 5" deep, glass. Figure frit cast by a lost wax process (cire perdue). The face and shelf were fuse cast in an open face mold. (photo by the author)

Lucartha Kohler, "Myth Maker," 16" high x 12" wide x 6" deep, glass.
(photo by the author)

One way to do this is by using a hammer to break up the glass. For safety sake, wrap the chunk in newspaper so that the flying fragments stay contained; also, wear safety glasses. Another method of breaking up glass is called fritting. A chunk of glass is placed in the kiln and the temperature brought up to 1000F. Turn off the kiln, with high-temperature gloves and a strong set of tongs reach into the kiln, pick up the chunk and drop it into a bucket of cold water. When the fritted chunk is at room temperature it can be tapped lightly with a hammer and should fall into small pieces.

The correct amount of glass for this process is best determined by weight or volume displacement, as the increased amount of glass required is deceiving.

A formula to figure a weight ratio for wax is: 1 part solid wax = 2.8 parts soda lime glass, or 3.6 parts of 40% lead glass

A formula to figure volume displacement (this will give you the correct amount of any type of glass to fill the mold cavity of the model):

1. Find a bucket large enough to totally submerge your model in water.
2. Fill the bucket with water (without the model) to a level high enough to completely cover the model and draw a line at the water level.
3. Submerge the model in the water and make a second line on the side of the bucket. (If your model is water-based clay, wrap the object in plastic wrap first as the clay will contaminate the water.)
4. Remove the model from the bucket and add enough glass to the water in the bucket to bring the water level back up to the second line.

Pate de verre

The first consideration for making a *pate de verre* object is the positive form or model. Most forms can be cast in *pate de verre*; however, if you are a novice, the easiest way to begin is to create a shallow flat form like a tile or a shallow bowl with thick walls, such as a soap dish. This type of mold process is called "open-face," meaning your negative mold cavity is exposed, and glass powders will be placed in the negative impressions.

Open face mold: An original or positive form needs to be modeled in a soft material, like water-based pottery clay or sculpture wax. Most any wax will do, microcrystaline wax such as "victory brown" is soft and is as easy to shape as clay. Other materials can be used to create a positive model; these are more complex mold procedures and will be explained later.

When the form is ready, a wall is built around the positive object. In mold making, this wall is called a "flask." This wall must be rigid enough to contain the plaster mold material before it sets up. Metal flashing, foam core board, plywood, PVC pipe and empty milk cartons all work well. Allow at least 1" around each side of the form and 2" above it. Tape all sides together with duct tape and secure the walls to your base with a hot glue gun. Next, seal around the base of the walls with wet clay (see Step 1 photo).

When the wall is secure, you begin to mix the mold material. Always wear a mask, as the silica flour can cause silicosis. The easiest and least costly mixture is equal ratio of plaster/silica. Combine 50% plaster (pottery plaster or plaster of Paris) and 50% silica flour (200-mesh flint). Both of these ingredients are available from pottery supply sources. The plaster/silica can be mixed together dry first or added alternately one measure at a time of each to the water. As with any plaster mixture, you begin with the water first. Pour cool water into a mixing bowl or bucket with half of the total volume you think is appropriate to fill the flask. Warm water sets up the plaster too quickly resulting in a weak mold. To judge the appropriate amount of mixture, calculate the amount of negative space between your object and the mold walls. As you gain experience, estimating the correct amount of water becomes easy.

Pate de verre: Step 1. Mold walls around clay positive edges sealed with clay.

Ready to mix! Add the dry mix to the water by gently sifting the powder onto the surface of the water until you have a dry island in the center of the water. Let it stand for four minutes, don't answer the phone now or it will be too late, plaster sets up quickly! If the island disappears into the water, add a bit more dry mixture until the island appears again. Begin to mix with your hands. If you're squeamish, a rubber spatula works well. The mixture should be the consistency of melted ice cream, without any lumps. Vibrate the bucket to bring any air bubbles to the surface.

The mixture is ready to pour into your mold cavity. (see Step 2). Pour slowly at first, in case your mold walls are not secure. A slow leak can soon become a tidal wave of liquid plaster. A little hint with any plaster mixture: Allow the spill to set up–it's much easier to clean up the mess. Also, using a spray vegetable oil in your bucket and on any tools and work surface helps facilitate clean-up. Never, never wash your hands, tools or buckets in your

Pate de verre: Step 2. Mix and pour the plaster/silica mold material.

sink unless you have a special plaster trap installed. You will become good friends with your plumber, as the plaster continues to set up and makes a major mess of drains and pipes. Keep a bucket of water next to your sink to pre-wash everything. When you need to empty the bucket, do so outdoors.

Once the plaster/silica mix is set up (it takes 20 minutes or so) and the mold is cool and rigid to the touch, you can remove the mold walls and begin to dig out the clay. Do this right away, while the clay is still soft, because it's much harder to remove once it dries. Be careful not to damage the walls of your mold with tools. After all of the clay is removed, clean the residue from the mold with a soft bristle brush. Acid brushes work well, the kind plumbers use for solder, available at any hardware store. If you have used wax, you can steam it out now in the top half of an old vegetable steamer used just for this purpose (see more

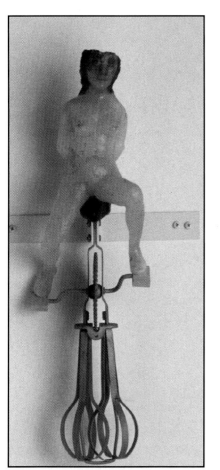

Anna Boothe, "Rider 1991," pate de verre, 23" high x 6" wide x 7" diameter. (photo courtesy of the artist)

detailed information under *"cire perdue"* or lost wax method of casting section). Now you have a refractory mold. Allow at least three days for the mold to air dry. The next step is choosing and preparing your glass and filling your mold.

Anna Boothe came to glass via a career as a pastry chef. The qualities in glass she liked were similar to those of cakes and pastries. They both required an oven and the decorating techniques were somewhat related. She builds very complex molds to cast bowls and figures using both clay and wax as positive models. The glass powders are packed into the molds as a paste mixed with a binder.

True *pate de verre* is a paste of glass that requires finely ground glass powders. There are any number of ways to buy or make glass powders. Kugler, Wiesenthalhutte, Zimmermann and Q colors are densely saturated color rods used by a large number of studio glassblowers. These colors are available as powders at a cost slightly under the national debt if you use them exclusively to cast with. They can, however, be mixed with a crystal or transparent base glass in much smaller amounts to achieve a desired color. Remember the important rule of compatibility of two or more glasses. One of the wonderful qualities of *pate de verre* is the subtle blending of colors possible. It's also a nightmare if the various colors used are not 100% compatible. They can fight with each other like spectators at an English soccer match.

Anna Booth, "Lady Bowl 1996," pate de verre, 10-1/2" high x 13" diameter. (photo courtesy the artist, photo by Eric Mitchell)

Anna Booth, "Lady Bowl" interior view 1996, pate de verre, 10-1/2" high x 13" diameter. (photo courtesy of the artist, photo by Eric Mitchell)

If you have a hot glass studio, or know some-one that does, you can use their base glass with the glass powders. They will know what powders are compatible with their glass formula. If you are buying cullet or using any other type of glass, then do a compatibility test to make sure the glass fits with the powders you want to use.

Bullseye Glass Co. in Portland, Oregon, has spent considerable time, energy and money to ensure the glass they sell as "compatible" really is compatible. All Bullseye sheet glasses are not necessarily compatible, so make sure the glass you buy is labeled "compatible." All of the frits they sell are compatible with each other and are available in powders and three grain sizes #1 fine is 0.2-1.2mm; #2 medium is 1.2-2.7mm; #3 coarse is 2.7-5.2mm.

Compatibility test: The simplest way to do this, if you only have a kiln available as a means to melt the glass, is to make a small casting. Make a mold in the shape of a disc and place a layer of the fritted base glass into the mold, Next, add a variety of color powders in a pie-wedge pattern over the fritted base glass. Fire the mold as you would a small casting. After the glass is cooled and the mold removed, you can test the results by using a polarizing filter. (See "Annealing" section)

Another test is called a pull test. For this test you will need a torch. A simple propane or mapp gas (available at hardware stores) can do the job. You will also need some glass rods and chunks of your base glass and the colors you wish to test. Begin by heating the end of a glass rod until it's soft and tacky, then pick up a small chunk of your base glass and slowly heat it until it is soft. Keep adding to the chunk of your base glass until you have a ball of molten glass about the size of a small marble. When the base glass is ready, begin to pick up a small amount of color, heating and melting it into the ball of molten glass. Do this step several times. When the two glasses are thoroughly melted together, take a pair of needle-nose pliers, grab a point on the ball of molten glass and pull it into a thin thread about 12" long. Hold it as straight as possible for several seconds, until the glass becomes rigid. If the two glasses are not compatible, you will see a bend in the thread. The test can also be done with strips of glass, using two pieces of glass side by side and melting them together. Remember to do only one color test at a time.

Glass preparation: Back to the *pate de verre* and preparation of the glass for casting. Since you want glass powders, most likely you will have to crush your own from chunks or particles. There are several ways of doing this. A cullet crusher can be purchased from Steinert Industries, or made by welding a steel collar to a base plate and then making a plunger-type hammer from a heavy steel cylinder. Stainless steel works best, as small amounts of rust can flake off into the glass if you use iron or steel. A regular old hammer works okay, but is messy. You can use an old blender or garbage disposer, but the blades tend to flake off bits of steel into the glass. They show up as tiny black specks in the finished piece. Rumor has it that you can use a magnet to remove these flakes from your frit, amazing! Be sure to protect your eyes; you're only issued one pair.

Once you've broken up the glass and washed it, sift the powders through a series of mesh screens rated according to particle size. If you are already in financial overwhelm and need to cut corners somewhere, you can use cheap plastic mesh screens made for needlepoint or window screening.

Now your molds are ready and your glass is ready. For true *pate de verre*, you want to mix your powders into a paste with a gum, alcohol and water solution. CMC, an organic cellulose gum, gum Arabic or gum terganth are all available from a pottery supply source. Mix the gum powders in a ratio of 1 table-spoon gum to 4 ounces of alcohol and 4 ounces of water. Thompson Enamels makes a product called "Klyr Fire" which is an organic cellulose gum mixed and ready to use.

Press the mixture into the mold cavity, over filling each color area as much as possible. When the glass melts, it shrinks and compresses a great amount. The gum binder burns off during the firing and holds the glass in place as the particles fuse together. (See steps 3 and 4 photos)

There are several ways to estimate the appropriate amount of glass you will need to fill your mold. Most types of glass require almost double the volume of the mold cavity. I often wonder where it all goes, especially the lead glasses. A shallow open-face mold is easiest to estimate. Mound the same amount of glass over the mold cavity equal to the amount you placed in it. Another way to determine the correct amount of glass is by water/volume displacement. (See "Frit Casting" section)

Load the kiln. Place your mold or molds on a kiln shelf in your kiln. If possible, place them so that they are visible through the peep holes in the side of the kiln. If your molds are large, it is a good idea to support all sides of them with soft fire brick. These bricks are available from most ceramic suppliers.

Ready to fire. A sacred ritual dance to the kiln spirits at this time might be appropriate!

Firing your kiln–ceramic kiln-sitter type kiln: Not recommended for castings larger than 1 cubic inch volume of glass.

1. Set timer for eight hours, put an 010 cone in the kiln-sitter device and prop lid open about 1″, turn all kiln switches on low for two hours. This slow rise in temperature allows any remaining moisture in the molds to burn off. If you have a pyrometer, it should read about 500F.

Step 3. Pack the various colored frit into the individual mold cavities.

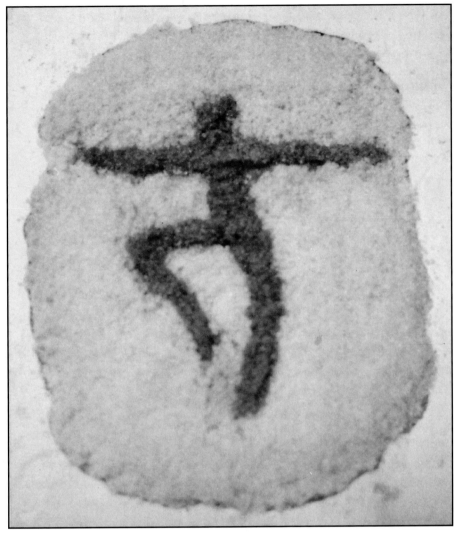

Step 4. Overfill with remaining glass.

2.   Close the lid and turn all switches to medium for one hour.
     This rise in temperature allows the chemical water to burn
     out of the plaster. This occurs at about 600F. Your pyrometer
     will eventually read 1000F.

3.   Turn all switches to high until the cone matures and turns off
     the kiln. The glass particles should be fused, depending on
     the type of glass you used. All lead glasses and most soft
     glasses like Bullseye fuse at about 1450F. Cone 010 matures at
     1650F and is a little higher than you need to fuse most soft
     glasses. Since it is not easy to hold an extended fixed temper
     ature or soak cycle in a ceramic kiln without a control unit,
     firing the kiln to a higher temperature gives the glass more
     time in the high temperature range filling all of the detail in
     your mold.

4. If you have good high temperature gloves, you can open the kiln 1" or so to allow some heat to escape. Do not let the temperature go below 1000F, as you will begin the annealing process at that temperature. Most ceramic kilns are well insu lated and will automatically cool down slowly enough to anneal small castings. If your pieces are slightly larger than a 1" cube of glass, you can try to turn one of the switches on low for several hours at the annealing temperature. To do this, put a higher cone in the kiln sitter and visually monitor the firing. A pyrometer is essential for this procedure. When your pyrometer reads 1650F, turn off all of the switches and allow the kiln to cool to 1000F. Turn one of the switches to low, check the temperature reading every 10 minutes to make sure that the kiln is maintaining a constant reading on the pyrometer.

This will take some practice to get a feel for how your kiln responds and where to set the switches. After you can maintain a temperature, you can gradually decrease it by turning the switch off for a little while, then back on again. Always be mindful of the temperature reading on the pyrometer. Sound tough? You might want to invest in a digital control unit to alleviate the necessity of constantly monitoring the kiln temperature.

Kiln with temperature controller: If you have a digital control unit, refer to your manual for specific instructions. See annealing chart for recommended time and temperature for a given thickness and type of glass. (See "Annealing" section)

Set point controller: If you have a set point controller, see "Annealing Chart" for recommended time and temperature for a given thickness and type of glass and follow procedures 1 through 7.

1. Set indicator dial on controller to 250F, allow to remain there for 30 minutes.
2. Set indicator dial to 500F, allow another 30 minutes.
3. Set indicator dial to 1000F, allow 60 more minutes.
4. Set indicator dial to 1650F, allow to soak at 1650F, for 60 minutes, or until the glass has filled the mold. Allow more time if your mold is large.
5. Set indicator dial to the appropriate annealing temperature for your glass. Allow to soak at this temperature for at least 60 minutes.
6. Set indicator dial to the appropriate strain point temperature for your glass, approximately 200F less than annealing point. If your glass object is thicker than a 1" cube, set dial in grad ual decreasing increments over a several hour period. This temperature decrease is the most critical part of the annealing procedure.

7. Set indicator dial to 0, turn off all switches if your object is
    small, otherwise repeat step 6 for several more hours.
    Allow kiln to reach room temperature.

Opening the kiln. This is something like a small child's Christmas morn-
ing–sometimes the suspense is unbearable. Resist the temptation to open the
kiln until it reaches room temperature. Pleasure? Disappointment? Don't worry
if your mold did not fill all the way. If the mold looks like it is in good condition
you can add more glass and fire it again. If possible, avoid removing the mold
from the kiln, as a once-fired mold is very fragile. If your mold filled, congratulations, you can remove it from the kiln. Handle it carefully. Remove the mold
material, ideally into a trash can. Fired mold material is very messy, wear a
mask for this job as the dust contains silica and is not healthy to breathe.

Before you wash your casting, make sure it is totally cool. If it is even
slightly warm, allow it to cool further before washing. A stiff brass brush, the
kind they sell for kitchen use, will help to clean off remaining mold material.
Excess glass, as well as sharp points and edges, can be ground off by hand or
machine. (See "Cold Working" section)

Completed demonstration model of "The Dancer." (photo by the author)

75

Fusing

Fused glass is one of the oldest forming methods. Fusing means to join two or more pieces of glass together with heat. The glassmakers of the Roman Empire made wonderful bowls by fusing together tiny pieces of fancy rod known as millifiore (thousand flowers). Even earlier, the Egyptians made tiny tiles and amulets by fusing together small chips of glass.

Because the nature of glass is that of a rigid liquid (and therefore full of stress), glass cannot be welded like metal. To join one piece of glass to another, the entire surface of both parts must be at the same temperature. It is possible to join very small pieces together with a torch (see "Lampworking" section). The best way to join larger pieces together is by fusing the parts in a kiln. The process can also be called laminating, although the term now generally refers to laminated safety glass where a thin layer of plastic is sandwiched between two pieces of glass.

Hemispherical bowl, late second century BC Italy or Eastern Mediterranean, 7.3 cm high x 12.4 cm diameter, 55.1.2. (photo courtesy of the Corning Museum of Glass)

Toots Zynsky, "Chaos Flaming Again," 1997, fused-glass threads, 12" high x 19-1/2" wide x 10" deep. (photo courtesy Elliot Brown Gallery)

Toots Zynsky, "Waterspout #14," 1994, blown wound threads, 30" high x 10" wide x 10" deep. (photo courtesy the artist, photo Robert Vinnedge)

Any type of glass can be fused, and there are many ways to approach fusing. Toots Zynsky began to hot wrap threads around her blown forms many years ago. She liked the threads. It wasn't long before the threads became the most important part of her work. Hand pulling tiny threads from a glass furnace became a very labor intensive pursuit so she enlisted the aid of a friend to build a thread-puller gadget. Now she pulls an endless rainbow of fine-colored threads from Italian glass rods and fuses, then slumps them into wonderfully complex shaped canvases.

Toots Zynsky, "A.W.O.L.," 1982, blown glass-fused threads, 8" high x 12" wide x 12" deep. (photo courtesy of the artist, photo by Ed Claycomb)

There are several important things to consider before fusing glass:

Consideration #1: The composition of the glasses to be fused must match. The best way to be sure of this is by using one type of glass made by the same manufacture such as Bullseye Compatibles. Very often, a manufacturer will produce more than one type of glass. Colored glasses present a problem as the oxides used to color the glass can affect the glass composition, unless the manufacturer takes steps to ensure compatibility, as Bullseye has done. Some other stained glass manufacturers such as Uroboros and Spectrum Glass are getting involved in the fusing business and are working toward having lines of glasses that fit. It's always best to test.

Klaus Moje, a German, now living in Australia, has worked for many years fusing rods of glass together to form intricately patterned bowls. He has also worked closely with Bullseye over the years to perfect their glass for fusing and his technique of combining multicolored rods and strips of glass into complex patterns that speak of the stark Australian landscape.

Plate and window glasses also fuse well to each other. Again, glass formulas differ from one company to the next. A very safe practice is to cut all of the pieces required from the same sheet of glass or buy several sheets at a time from your supplier. Better yet, recycle! In most areas of the country, plate glass is not a recyclable material to municipal trash systems. Your local

Klaus Moje, "Mosaic Bowl," 1980, 7.1 cm high x 32.4 cm wide x 24.8 cm diameter, 82.3.33. (photo courtesy the Corning Museum of Glass)

auto/window/mirror dealer generally has remnants of broken plate glass from windows. They will usually sell it very cheap or even free. Just ask! The author's series of works titled "Harmony's Realm of Light" was made from recycled plate glass windows, gathered over a period of 10 years from many sources. Broken windows are the unfortunate victims of crime in our urban environments but good sources of usable glass.

Compatibility test, soft (stained) glass
1. Cut a square piece of your base glass, preferably clear.
2. Cut smaller pieces of colors or other clears you wish to test.
3. Make a diagram of your color test pieces on a sheet of paper.
4. Place the test pieces on the sheet of base glass according to the diagram and attach with a dot of Elmer's glue.
5. Place the glass in a kiln and fire to about 1450F
6. Allow to cool to room temperature and remove. If you see any visible cracks around the color chips, it's not even close. You will want to look through polarized film to determine stress not visible to the naked eye. Stress tester (see "Annealing" section)

Consideration #2: The temperature required to fuse glass depends on the type of glass used and the viscosity of the glass as it is melting. A wide range of effects from a light tack to a total melt are possible in all types of glass. Following are some temperature suggestions for various types of glasses.
- Lead glass and soft Italian glass (i.e., Effetre/formerly Moretti) begins to soften/tack at 1200F and melt at 1350F-1400F.
- Soda/lime soft glass (i.e., Bullseye etc.) soften/tack 1300F and melt at 1650F.
- Plate/window glass including colored-plate, soften/tack 1350F and melt at 1650F. These temperatures are just a guide. Each kiln fires according to its own personality and it may take some trial and error to get to know your kilns idiosyn crasies.

When making test firings, try different areas of the kiln and record the information. All kilns have a wide-range of temperature variants. Most kilns fire hotter toward the top. If the shelves are stacked, work placed in the center of the kiln that is buried under other shelves will fire much cooler. Fiber board and fiber blanket are not as dense as a kiln shelf so it will heat and cool more rapidly. Allow for this heat differential in calculating time and temperature for a firing cycle. A good pyrometer is a valuable aid in any type of glass firing, and it's a must in slumping and critical fusing work. If you fall madly in love with the fusing process, investing in a kiln designed just for fusing with elements on the top is worthwhile. The top radiant heat is evenly distributed to all of the glass pieces at the same time on the kiln shelf.

Consideration #3: To set up the fusing project for firing, you will need a surface suitable to build your fusing project. Ideally, a coated kiln shelf works best, as a design can be assembled right on the shelf and not be disturbed as it is placed in the kiln for firing. For small pieces such as jewelry parts both soft and hard firebrick can be used. These surfaces will require a shelf primer coating.

If commercial kiln wash or shelf primer is not working, try the following recipe to make 1 pint of high-fire shelf primer: in a 1 quart container, add dry ingredients of 8 ounces of kaolin and 8 ounces of silica (200 mesh). Fill the container with water and mix thoroughly–mixture should be about like heavy whipping cream before whipping. Brush an even coat with a broad bristle brush (Chinese multi-stem hake brushes work great). When the coating is thoroughly dry, it can be sanded lightly with fine sandpaper to remove traces of brush strokes. Each time a kiln shelf is used for a fusing project, it should be checked for any cracks in the shelf and any flaking off of the coating. When recoating, it's a good idea to remove all of the old primer with a broad blade putty knife, then recoat.

If an available kiln shelf is not large enough, a sheet of ceramic refractory fiberboard can be used. Most refractory manufacturers make the board in a variety of thickness, as well as a line of fiber papers. Fiber board or paper does not need to be coated with kiln wash; however, it needs to be fired first to about 1200F to burn off the organic binder. The fumes are not toxic, but they smell awful so the kiln area should be well ventilated.

Other sheet products, Refractory Sheet Type 100 (RS-100) and Refractory Sheet Type DD (RSDD) made by Zircar are alumina composite materials. They are expensive but will last a long time if handled carefully. RS100 is very thin and needs to be used with a support or on a kiln shelf to prevent warping. Most glasses will not stick to the material; if sticking should occur, a layer of ceramic paper, such as Zircar's ASPA-1, can act as a parting agent. Zircar recommends using its Rigidizer/Hardner each time the sheet is fired.

Consideration #4. Supports or mold walls to contain the glass are important, especially when firing above the softening point of a glass. When several layers of glass are stacked together for a full fuse, a wall will prevent the glass from running all over the place. Any material capable of withstanding high temperatures can be used. Bisque-fired clay, hard and soft fire brick, steel and stainless steel all require a separator; fiber board and ceramic fiber paper do not.

Cutting strips of plate glass to fuse.

Molds built around plate-glass in kiln to fuse.

Consideration #5. Glass can be stacked vertically, as well as horizontally. Glass, when molten, follows Isaac Newton's rule of gravity. All that goes up, must come down. When stacking layers of glass in a vertical pattern, the stack must be sustained with a strong support, otherwise the weight of the glass will push the wall away when it begins to soften and move. Often, there is little temperature difference between full fusing (when all of the separate pieces are homogenous) and kiln casting, which is essentially fusing bits of frit or cullet together in a mold.

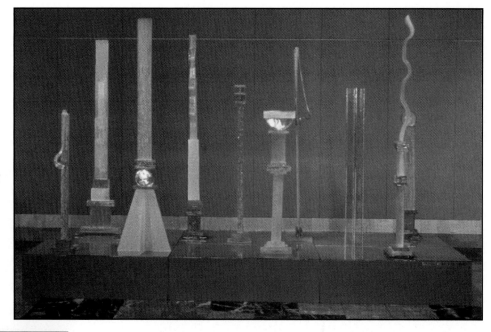

Lucartha Kohler, "Harmony's Realm of Light," Installation, University City Science Center, Philadelphia PA, 1990, glass, 8 feet high x 12 feet wide x 4 feet deep. (photo by the author)

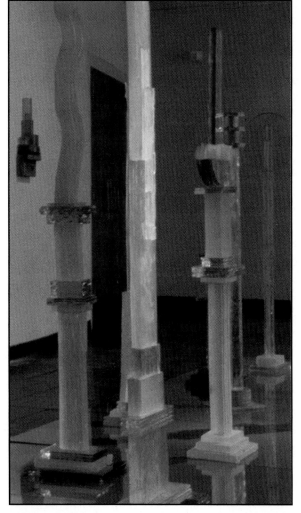

"Harmony's Realm of Light," 1992 at the Morris Museum. (photo by the author)

"Harmony's Realm of Light," 1997 at Washington Square. (photo by the author)

Making a Millifiori Bowl

To make a bowl much like the Roman glassmakers made 2,000 years ago, you will need to buy or make some millifiori rod. The Italian glass company, Effetre (formerly Moretti) makes and sells these rods, frit and the millifiori pieces by the bag. If you happen to have a friend in the glass art business, they can make some for you.

1. Cut rods into 1/4" segments with a pair of nipper pliers.
2. Prepare surface and walls to fuse against. Clay flower pot saucers or cut-off tops coated with shelf primer work great.
3. Arrange millifiori in a pattern on the kiln shelf. Make sure they touch each other as the segments will bead-up as the glass softens and pull apart during the firing process.
4. Fire kiln to 1450F for Effetre, higher for most other glasses. Anneal according to thickness of the glass.
5. After plate is cool, clean with a wire brush and grind or sand any rough areas. Place in a shallow bowl form to slump.

Millifiori bowl set up in flower pot ring to fuse plate.

Fused plate with Bullseye compatibles

1. Cut base plate according to size and place on a kiln shelf. Cut pattern pieces and arrange on base plate. Elmer's glue will hold the pieces in place. Layer colors for interesting effects.
2. Fire kiln. 1550F will fuse the layers to a full-fuse in most kilns. Anneal according to thickness of glass.
3. Clean, when cool and place in mold to slump.

Bullseye compatible sheet glass to cut for fusing project.

Glass cut and ready to fuse.

Slumping

When glass is heated, it goes through varying degrees of softness before becoming a liquid. In this soft state, glass can be formed in a variety of ways. Historically, the technique sometimes referred to as sagging was used to flatten the large cylinders blown for window glass. During the late 19th century, the technique of bending flat panes of stained glass was extensively used by Tiffany for his lamp shades, and large panes of glass were bent for Victorian bow front cabinetry. Industry today uses many forms of bending and slumping glass to make automobile windshields, large architectural panels, doors, windows, tableware and electrical components.

The nature of glass, when soft or molten, is to follow gravity's force downward. Heat, plus gravity, work to provide some very interesting forms. An endless variety of shapes can be obtained (depending on the type and shape mold or forming device, as well as the temperature to which the glass is fired). Any material, providing it can withstand the necessary temperatures, can be used to support the glass in the kiln. The glass is gradually heated to the softening temperature, allowed to bend and then is slowly cooled or annealed. Control and skill, combined with the excitement of the unexpected, are aspects of the process of slumping glass.

The challenge of working

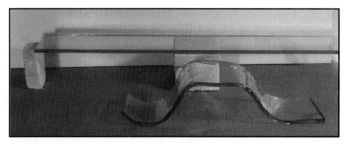

A piece of plate glass is set up so that just the very edge is supported by the brick on the end. If glass is only on one support, it can crack when heated in the kiln. (photo courtesy of the author)

Fused millifiori plate on bisque-fired-clay bowl form for slumping. (photo courtesy of the author)

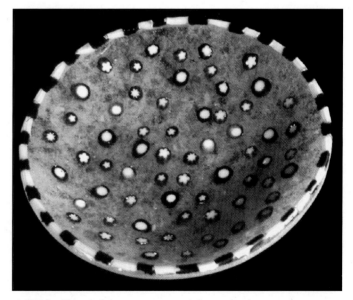

Millifiori bowl. (photo courtesy of the author)

85

with glass in this manner is directly involved with the amorphous character of glass. One can freeze a moving mass of glass in a permanent state of suspension. Mary Shaffer does just that with her tool series. She uses found metal objects, such as hooks, that look like they belong to a construction site. These metal objects are placed in a kiln with glass. The kiln is turned on. At the precise moment, when the glass bends over the metal, the kiln is stopped to freeze the glass in place.

The types of glass used for slumping are as diverse as the possible forming methods. Industrial plate glass, colored flat glass, laboratory glass, commercial or hand-blown glass all slump according to their initial forms, the system used to support the glass and the firing temperature of the kiln. Free slumping, supporting only a portion of the glass object in the kiln, requires diligent monitoring and critical temperature control. A few minutes or a few degrees in temperature can mean success or failure. Over-firing can result in a pool of molten glass.

Mary Shaffer, "Red Wheel," 1996, 25" high x 14" wide x 5" deep, glass and metal. (Collection Museum Bellerive, Switzerland, courtesy of the artist, photo by George Erml)

Mary Shaffer, "Tool-Wall" detail, 1995, metal and glass. (photo courtesy of the artist)

Sydney Cash uses very fine wire to support his glass in the kiln. The glass that is not supported flows into delicate folds as the kiln goes above the softening temperature of the glass. It requires diligent monitoring to stop the glass flow at just the right moment.

The first important consideration when planning a slumping project is the size of kiln you have available. It is important that the piece of glass move freely within the firing chamber, without touching the walls of the kiln or anything else other than the intended support system. Every surface the glass contacts, especially kiln shelves and furniture, must be coated with a separator such as kiln wash.

The next step to consider is the method of forming the shape you want. Ask yourself—what am I making? Then—how do I go about constructing it? For instance, a bowl can be slumped into a mold, over a mold or free slumped from a ring support. The handkerchief vase made popular by Italian glassmakers, for example, is slumped over a support made by pouring plaster/silica mold material into a paper cup, placing a square piece of flat glass over it and allowing gravity and heat to pull the glass downward to create the effect of a stiffly starched handkerchief.

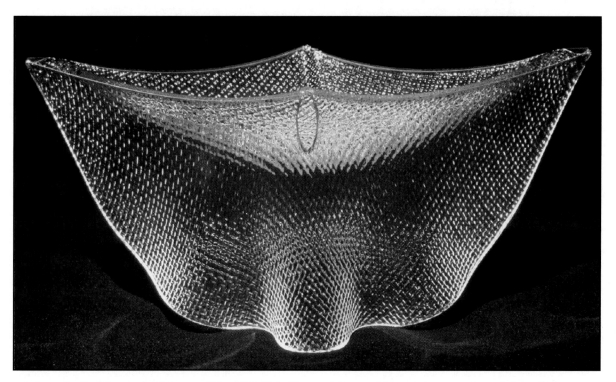

Sydney Cash, "Suspended Diamond Bowl," 1996, 20 cm x 37 cm x 18 cm. (photo courtesy of the artist)

Plates and shallow bowls are best slumped into a mold. The mold can be made from bisque-fired clay, stainless steel, iron or even plaster/silica. Note that the plaster/silica will usually break down after one firing.

Metal molds and supports: When using metal as a mold or support, the softening temperature of the metal must be considered. The approximate slumping range for most soft glasses is 1250F-1350F and for plate glass 1350F-1450F. Most mild steel alloys, stainless steel, copper, bronze and brass can be used. Galvanized steel should be avoided because of the toxic fumes emitted from the zinc coating. (See "Health Hazards" section)

Sydney Cash, "Purity of Form," 1996, glass, mixed media, 12" x 10" x 9". (photo courtesy of the artist)

Here are approximate melting temperatures for metals:

Aluminum 1250F
Brass 1900F
Bronze 1900F
Cast iron 2100F
Copper 1900F
Lead 600F
Steel 2800F

Some metals expand and contract more than the glass does, especially steel. Stainless steel can be slumped over or into and works best because it does not oxidize when heated. Stainless steel bowls from your kitchen make great molds for slumping into. All metal must be coated with a separator as hot glass will stick to hot metal.

When the glass goes through firing and annealing, so does the metal. Annealed metal is very soft and will bend with very little effort. It can be re-hardened by heating and quenching in water.

It is important to remember the expansion coefficient of the glass you are using when using any mold material. If the glass should expand and get hung-up in an undercut or over the lip of a mold, it will surely crack as it cools and contracts. Also, when slumping over a rigid form such as clay or metal, the glass will crack as it cools because the mold is stronger than the glass. Coating the surface of a rigid mold with a thick layer of separator will minimize this to some extent. The glass will move freely over the surface of the separator and compress against the softer material as it contracts.

Refractory materials as molds and supports: The availability of new precast refractory ceramic fiber materials (RCF) has greatly increased the ability of an artist to slump difficult and complex shapes. Both refractory board and blanket come in an assortment of thickness from 1/4" to 2". Ceramic fiber papers are even thinner and can be draped and molded over a support or used as a separator on a kiln shelf. These materials are very soft, are easily cut, carved or pressed into a shape and compress easily with the contraction of the glass. Glass may be placed over these forms or supported in various ways by propping. There is a slight texture, according to the type of glass used and the temperature to which it is fired, and this texture will be reproduced. Coating with a separator of dry whiting will help minimize this rough surface. Be careful handling the materials, as the dust created is not healthy to breath; a mask or respirator is a must.

89

Zircar makes a product Refractory Sheet Type DD (RSDD) formally known as Luminary Moldable Sheet. This material has the ability to become pliable when wet and can be formed into a variety of shapes. It will retain the shape when dry; however, once fired it cannot be reshaped.

Soft firebrick: Soft firebrick also works well as a support, again a separator such as kiln wash is required. As the brick is rigid and does not compress, it's important to align the glass so that it does not get hung-up or it will crack.

Castable refractory molds: A simple relief mold without undercuts can be made from lightweight castable refractory material like Kast-O-Lite 25 (from A.P. Green) or Hydracon 24 (from J.H. France). Other refractory manufacturers have similar products and can be identified by comparing to A.P. Green's product line. If handled carefully, this type of mold can hold up for many firings. With this material, it is necessary to begin with a model. This model can be of almost any material, but moist clay works the best. To prepare for the mold process, place the model on a base and make a retaining wall. This wall is called a flask and could be of metal flashing, plastic, clay or wood. All joints should be sealed with moist clay to prevent leakage. A release agent, such as Vaseline, silicone or green soap, is brushed on all surfaces that come in contact with the castable refractory material.

Mold #1: 80%-90% Kast-O-Lite 25 or comparable product; 10-20% plaster, plaster of Paris, molding plaster or pottery plaster. The addition of 10-20% plaster to the dry mixture will help the slurry set up faster and pick up any fine detail in the model. To mix the castable refractory, you begin with cool water in a bucket–about one-third of the volume needed to fill the mold flask. Sift the dry ingredients into the water until there is a dry island in the middle. Allow to settle for several minutes, then stir. You want the mixture to be rather thick as too much water reduces the strength of the mold. Vermiculite flakes in the refractory will float to the surface, so continue stirring until most of them settle. Pour the mixture into the mold flask and allow to set several hours or overnight. Remove the flask walls and the positive model carefully; allow to dry thoroughly, at least a week. The mold must be fired first to 1000F then allowed to cool to room temperature. The mold is then coated with high-fire kiln wash before using.

Mold #2: A more expensive mold, but one that lasts for many, many firings. It is made from a denser refractory castable like A.P. Green's Mizzou or Greencast 94 or 97. The mold is made like the Kast-O-Lite formula; however, I recommend using a U.S. Gypsum product, hydroperm, instead of plaster, as it already contains some refractory material. There can't be any undercuts in the model or any way glass can get hung up in the mold. Because this type of mold is much denser than the lightweight castable mold mixture, you must allow a way for gases to escape when firing. Broom straws or waxed threads can be cast directly into the mold or tiny holes can be drilled after the mold has dried and been fired. Allow a hole for every 2 square inches of mold surface. This mold must also be prefired, then coated with high fire kiln wash. I have molds made from this formula that have lasted 10 years. One very large slumping mold has been stored outside for that long in snow, ice and rain. It still works fine! You can use this type of mold for casting, as long as the object can be dumped out of the mold when the glass has cooled.

There are lots of unexplored mold material possibilities in the castable refractory and ceramic-fiber refractory industries. When trying a new material, it is important to find out its maximum and continuous use temperature ratings and whether it is wetting or non-wetting to molten glass. If it is wetting to glass, you must use a separator.

Clay molds: Clay molds work well for slumping plates and bowls. You can even use shallow terra-cotta flower pots. When making your own, the clay may be slip-cast, hand-built or thrown on a potter's wheel. Allow the clay object to dry, then bisque fire to cone 08. Before using, spray or brush on several coats of kiln wash. I don't recommend glazed clay objects, as the glaze is a glass, and–even though coated with a separator–your glass could stick to the glazed surface and crack.

Plaster molds: The difficulty with any plaster mold when exposed to extreme temperatures is that the plaster begins to break down at 600F. Thus the mold will generally hold up for one firing, sometimes cracking. The only advantage of this type mold for slumping is surface detail. The plaster does not need a separator, imparting a good clean surface on most glasses. (See Plaster/Silica mold directions in "Molds" section)

Now that you have a mold, the type and shape of the glass is also important.

Cutting glass: First things first–always wear safety glasses! Cutting glass takes practice. Start with a good quality glass cutter and keep it well oiled with cutting oil or kerosene. Use a wood guide, metal can nick the cutting wheel and cause an uneven score. Hold the cutter between your index and middle fingers, supported from behind with your thumb. Place the cutting wheel

91

on the glass, holding the cutter at a 45-degree angle to the glass. Apply a steady even pressure and drag the cutter along the wooden guide, the entire length of the piece of glass. Examine the score closely, it should be a continuous unbroken line. If it looks okay, grab the shortest piece with breaking pliers and snap away from the score line. If this motion does not break the glass, gently tap along the score line with the ball end of the cutter. You will begin to see a crack develop, then keep tapping all along the score line until the glass separates. If this does not work, turn the glass over and make a new score on the other side. Never go back into a cut a second time. Also, if you wait too long before you try to separate a score, it will heal itself; turn the glass over and try again.

Cutting glass. (Photos courtesy of the author)

This technique works well for glass up to 1/4″ thick. To cut thicker glass, make your score line, then tap the line from below with a ball peen hammer. Don't be afraid to get tough. Tap all along the score line, then place the score line on the table edge and snap. Another method is to gently heat the score line with a propane torch. When the line is warm, apply cold water along the line. An empty dish detergent bottle works well. Be careful, this technique is tricky. If the glass gets too hot, it will crack where you don't want it to.

This information is just to get you going, there are some good stained glass books with instructions on how to cut glass. You also might want to hang out at your local glass dealer's shop to pick up bits of information—he or she may help you.

Guidelines for placing the objects in a kiln

1. If the glass is to be slumped over a mold, it should be large enough to extend well beyond the edges of the mold or support. Any excess can be trimmed after firing.

2. When slumping a large piece of glass over a narrow form, you need to support the glass at several points. The pressure and weight of unsupported glass will create stress as the glass is heated, causing it to break (see photo).

3. If the glass is to be slumped into a rigid mold, it is important that the glass does not extend beyond the edges (see photos). As mentioned, the glass will get hung-up on the edges of the mold and very likely crack the entire piece. The same principle applies to deep undercuts.

4. A drop-out form for free slumping can be made of metal, clay or RCF board. It can be a ring, square, rectangle or free-form shape. The form is supported by kiln stilts or firebrick at least 3" higher than the intended slump (see photos). This process requires careful monitoring. You must stop the process at just the right moment, or the glass will continue moving until it reaches the floor and then some. Keep good records of firing times and temperatures. If you are doing the same shape and type of glass, your results can be predictable. Caution! Just when you think you have a handle on things...something goes awry. Don't despair, it happens to everyone once in awhile.

Firing the glass: The type and thickness of the glass and the support system both determine the firing schedule, especially for increasing temperature. Window glass and colored cathedrals may be heated rather quickly. Heavier plate glass and cast forms should be heated very slowly. A conservative estimate for the rise in temperature for glass less than 1/4" thick would be 500F in the first hour, then the remainder of the temperature rise can occur more rapidly. For heavier glass, double the time for the first 500F. The next 500F increase should take another hour. Once past the annealing point of your glass, a more rapid increase is possible.

The temperature at which the glass begins to bend is referred to as the softening point. This will vary, depending on the type of glass used. Soft glasses, such as lead glass and colored cathedrals, will begin to soften between 1050F and 1100F; window glasses begin to soften at about 1250F. A wide range of bending can occur within the next 200F. The maximum temperature for slumping colored glasses should be 1350F, and 1400F for window glasses. When glass is held at a high temperature for a prolonged period of time, the surface tends to devitrify. Devitrified glass is characterized by crystals that cause surface imperfections. The best way to avoid that is to rapidly cool the kiln to below the softening point. This can be done by opening the lid and allowing some heat to escape. Make sure you are wearing good gloves.

As glass softens and becomes viscous, there are degrees within the viscosity that can be controlled. The size of the piece of glass also affects the rate of speed the piece slumps at a given temperature. Gravity will pull large unsupported areas down faster than supported areas. It is advisable to open the kiln slightly or look through peep holes to check the progress of the slump.

An exciting and challenging technique is working directly in the kiln with the glass as it is slumping. By reaching into the kiln with tools and manipulating the glass when it is soft, many interesting forms can be created. Be sure to turn off the kiln before you reach in there. Wear adequate protection; it gets mighty hot. Also, remember to compensate for the heat loss in the kiln if the lid or door is open for any length of time.

Fused Bullseye plate project ready to slump in drop-out slump mold. (photo courtesy of the author)

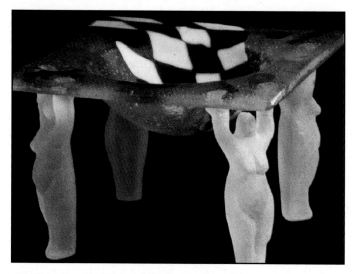

Goddess Bowl with fused Bullseye plate. (photo courtesy of the author)

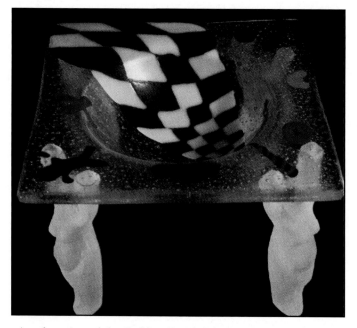

Another view of the Goddess Bowl. (photo courtesy of the author)

Firing schedule for slumping

Ceramic kiln with kiln sitter:
I recommend a good pyrometer: It will save you time and money.

> Cone 019: 1250F, lead glass, soft soda-lime
> Cone 018: 1325F, most stained glasses
> Cone 017: 1400F, bending window and plate glass
> Cone 016: 1450F, slumping window and plate

1. Place appropriate cone in kiln sitter device and press in button to activate. If you have a timer, set to three to four hours depending on the thickness of your glass. Close the lid and prop open about 1". Remove any plugs from peep holes.
2. Turn all switches to low for one hour. If your kiln appears to be heating too rapidly, adjust switches accordingly. You don't want to exceed a 500F increase in temperature during the first hour.
3. Turn all switches to medium for one hour and close lid and peep holes. You should have reached 1000F by this time, well above the strain and annealing point for most glasses.
4. Turn all switches to high. At this point in the firing cycle, the glass can be heated quickly. The time can vary according to kiln size, age and condition of elements, as well as the number of molds and kiln shelves. Too many variables!! Not to worry, you will learn the distinct characteristics of your own kiln in time.
5. Keep an eye on the progress, either by looking in the peep holes or carefully opening the lid (with high temperature gloves). You can stop the firing at any time by turning the switches off. The kiln will shut off when the cone bends and trips the device or the timer runs out of time.
6. Annealing cycle. The normal cooling down of a well insulated kiln is sufficient to anneal glass up to 1/4" thick. If your glass is thicker than that, I recommend a digital programmer, as it is very difficult to hand ramp-down by turning switches on and off. It's impossible without a pyrometer.
7. Allow kiln to reach room temperature before opening

Firing schedule for digital programmer, accumulated time
1. 0-500F for one hour (60 minutes total).
2. 500F-1000F for one hour (120 minutes total)
3. 1000F slump temp (see list above for appropriate temperature for type of glass) for one hour (180 minutes total)
4. Slump temp, 1000F or appropriate annealing temperature for type of glass for 30 minutes, your kiln may take longer to drop back in temperature (210 minutes total)
5. 1000F (or annealing temp) for one hour (270 minutes total)
6. 1000F-800F (or strain point) for four hours (510 minutes total), especially for glass 1/4" thick to 1/2" thick; for thicker glass, see chart for annealing cast glass
7. Turn off kiln and allow to reach room temperature before opening

Surface Decoration

The desire to enhance the surface of a glass object was developed in early Egypt. Beads and vessels produced in the New Kingdom were often decorated by winding multicolored threads of glass on the surface of the bead. Some evidence of lapidary (gem cutting) techniques are also found to have existed in this early period of glass history. Gilding, using metallic gold and silver to decorate the surface of glass objects, appeared during the first century AD, most likely in Rome.

The Islamic world of the eighth through the 10th century made many significant contributions to both the forms glass would assume and the manner it was decorated. The use of vitreous paints, enamels and lusters first appeared in Syria, followed by the African Moors use of silver stains. Gilding with gold and silver, the earlier Roman technique, was incorporated into the Byzantine decorative style. The flourishing trade routes of the Turkish Empire spread Byzantine glass worldwide and strongly influenced the early direction of Venetian and European glass.

By the 12th century, European glassmakers were beginning to color their glass. In 1144, Abby Suger incorporated the first colored and painted stained glass windows in the construction of the Abby Church of St. Denis, Paris, France. The term "stained glass" is derived from the process of staining glass for windows used extensively in Europe during the 14th and 15th centuries. The technique traveled to America in the 18th century and is still in use today. The staining of glass depends on the action of metallic salts altering the molecular structure of the glass, thus changing its color. The limited range of pot colors available at the time made silver staining a viable means of obtaining a multicolored palate.

The term **glass painting** usually refers to the technique of drawing and painting on the surface of glass to be installed in a leaded glass panel. These paints were used to control light transmission, alter color and add texture to the glass. They were often used to create a three-dimensional effect on a two-dimensional surface, most often to include details where lead lines would be awkward such as facial expressions and drapery folds. Paint for glass consists of finely ground glass or frits, metallic and refractory oxides and a flux. The paint melts at a lower temperature than the glass when fired, creating a permanent bond. The colors available range from blue-gray through browns and blacks and

97

can be applied thinly as a wash or heavy opaque as line drawing.

Low-fire glass enamels are glass colors, but not the same as glass paints. They are finely ground glass, metallic oxides and a flux; however, they fuse with the surface of the glass at a lower temperature than the glass paints. There is more variety of color possible, but they are less stable than the glass paints when exposed to time and the elements. They have been used primarily as a paint to decorate the surface of glass objects. There are both opaque and transparent colors available commercially with an almost infinite palette.

High-fire glass enamels are glass colors made much the same way as low-fire enamels; however, the fluxing agent melts at a higher temperature. They are sometimes referred to as China paints and are used to decorate glazed ceramic and porcelain ware. These paints are ideal for use in slumping and fusing as they melt at a higher temperature. They also can be incorporated in some blown glass techniques.

Today, there is a growing number of artists using these enamels on glass objects, as one would paint on a canvas. The potential use of these pigments is limitless: The concept of glass as canvas is just beginning to be explored by artists seeking challenging and creative ways of expressing their inner vision.

Paint for glass consists of finely ground glass, metallic oxides and a flux. The paint melts at a lower temperature than the glass when fired creating a bond. The terms "glass paints" and "glass enamels" are not synonymous. The term glass paint usually refers to the technique of drawing and painting on the surface of glass to be installed in a leaded glass panel. The colors range from blue-gray through to brown or black and can be applied thinly as a wash or as a heavy and opaque line drawing. They are often used to create a three-dimensional effect on a two-dimensional surface.

Glass paints are available commercially. They are usually available in the form of a powder. This powder is mixed with water and gum Arabic to the desired consistency. The techniques of handling the paints are similar to those of handling watercolors. Some skill is required to perfect this technique, as there is a close relationship to painting and drawing. For more specific information, I refer you to a book by Albinas Elskus, *The Art of Painting on Glass.*

J. Kenneth Leap paints on glass in the traditional sense of glass painting. His subject matter, however, is often not traditional. He sometimes paints on blown surfaces, as well as fusing layers of painted surfaces together in solid forms.

J. Kenneth Leap, "The King and Queen of Frogs," 1995, 6-3/4" x 3-1/2" x 2". (collection of Judge David Schepps, courtesy of the artist)

J. Kenneth Leap, "The Joker," 1989, 18" x 24". (photo courtesy of the artist)

Glass Enamels

Low-fire glass enamels or glass colors are also finely ground glass, metallic oxides and a flux; however, they fuse with the surface of the glass at a lower temperature than the glass paints. There is more variety of color possible, but they are less stable than the glass paints when exposed to time and the elements. There are both opaque and transparent colors available commercially with an almost infinite palette. The techniques used to apply the enamels on glass are similar to those of painting on glass. Silk-screen or airbrush techniques are also possible alternatives. In fact, any manner in which one can apply the paint to the surface of the glass would be possible.

It is advisable to fire individual colors separately; however, as a new application may lift off a previously applied layer. The colors made by Rausche are of high quality. They have been supplying the glass industry for more than 75 years. It is likely that any problem you may encounter has been presented to them and a solution is readily available. I have found their glass colors, as well as Drakenfeld glass colors, mix well to obtain subtle shades of a given color. They can be made more opaque by adding white pigment or more transparent by adding soft flux. Soft flux, a Drakenfeld glass color, is a low-melting flux compatible with most soft glasses. A number of other companies make enamels and are listed in "Supply Sources." It is important to follow each manufacturer's recommended firing directions to ensure success. (There is a special series of colors available for borosilicate glasses.) The soft flux can be used to lower the melting temperature of most higher fluxing ceramic pigments. For instance, by adding soft flux to over-glaze colors (1400F) you can lower the firing range to that of glass colors (1050F-1100F.) Ceramic underglazes or stains may also be mixed with soft flux. Test first if you plan to try these mixtures, as glaze compositions vary greatly.

If you are ambitious and concerned with the chemistry of color composition, you can mix your own enamels. I recommend extensive testing before deciding on any one formula for a specific color. Low-firing frits (fluxes) are available from ceramic supply companies. They may be mixed with colorants (metal oxides) at an approximate ratio of 90% flux to 10% colorant. (Cobalt and chromium are intense, so start with only 1%-2%.)

This is a typical formula for an easily fusible glass flux[1]:

- 60 parts red lead
- 30 parts boric acid
- 10 parts silica

This is thoroughly melted in a crucible and poured into water to cool. It is then finely ground in a ball mill. An adjustment may be required to match this formula to your glass. To increase the fusing temperature, add more lead. To decrease the fusing temperature add more silica. The metallic oxides used as colorants will, in some instances, act as a flux to lower the fusing temperature. Test each adjustment with your base glass.

The metal oxides used to create specific colors are also available in silicate form from ceramic supply companies. Following is a list of the colorants and the approximate colors they produce. Again, I recommend extensive testing, as this information should serve only as a rough guide.

Colorant	**Color**
Chromium oxide	greens, yellows, oranges
Cobalt oxide	blues, purples
Cobalt carbonate	blues, purples
Copper carbonate	turquoise, greens, reds
Black copper oxide	blacks
Gold chloride	pinks, reds
Iron oxide	browns, red-browns, blacks
Magnesium oxide	purples, blacks
Silver nitrate	yellows, ambers

Firing

Any electric kiln can be used to fire enamels on glass. If you're using a cone system, cone 022 is appropriate for the pigment to fuse to the surface of the glass. A pyrometer is less accurate. Depending on the accuracy of your instrument, 1050F-1100F should be sufficient to fuse the pigment. When firing glass, the first 500F increase in temperature is critical. Too rapid an increase will crack the glass. Also, it is important to vent the kiln during these first 500F to allow the fumes to escape. To vent, open all the peep holes and prop the lid open at least 1". The lid may be lowered and the peep holes closed when all the smoke and odor have disappeared. Continue firing until the desired temperature is achieved. If you are checking your piece visually, the surface of the enamel will appear glossy when properly fired.

The normal cooling down of the kiln is sufficient to anneal glass up to 1/4" thick. See the section on "Annealing" for more information. Do not open the kiln until it has reached room temperature. It is necessary to coat the kiln floor and shelves with a separator. I found kiln wash alone is satisfactory, but an additional coat of dry whiting sifted over the kiln wash works best. You will need to replace the whiting after each firing. Take extreme care not to get any of the whiting on the surface of your enamels, as it will bond permanently to the glass.

Glass Stains

The term "stained glass" is derived from the process of staining glass for windows used extensively in Europe in the 14th and 15th centuries. The staining of glass is a process which involves ion exchange and migration. The stains are part of the glass, but the effect is only on the surface. Silver nitrate mixed with ochre or clay and fired will produce a yellow or orange stain. Copper salts will produce a reddish stain. In reduction firing, stains can produce luster effects, although these effects are difficult to control. For more detailed technical information on the use of silver stains, *The Technique of Stained Glass* by Patrick Reyntiens is quite comprehensive.

Fired Precious Metals

Gilding, or the use of metallic gold or silver, is one of the oldest methods of surface decorating. The pure metal is used in powdered form and incorporated with a flux and lavender oil. Formulas for the preparation of these metallic coatings are very elaborate, reminiscent of the old alchemist's "secret elixirs." However, gold, silver and platinum are readily available commercially. These fired coatings are very expensive as they are made from pure metals. The metals, available commercially in liquid form, are applied in a very thin coating to the surface of the glass object and fired. In addition to the metals, there is a wide variety of metallic lusters in a shimmering rainbow of colors. Some of the lusters fire opaque and appear as polished metal, while others barely coat the glass with a pearly haze. Some very interesting effects can be obtained by combining these lusters with the transparency of glass. As with any new or newly directed technique, much experimentation and investigation needs to be accomplished. The price of these firing metals fluctuates with the price of precious metals.

There is also a wide range of metallic lusters available in liquid form. "Hanovia" liquid bright metals and liquid lusters are available from ceramic supply companies. Most of these lusters are made for use on ceramic materials and are meant to be fired to cone 017-019 (1450F). This temperature is within the slumping and fusing range of most glasses. To lower the fusing temperature for a glass firing, add a flux. Hanovia makes a series of lusters in some metallic colors plus gold, silver and platinum preparations just for glass.

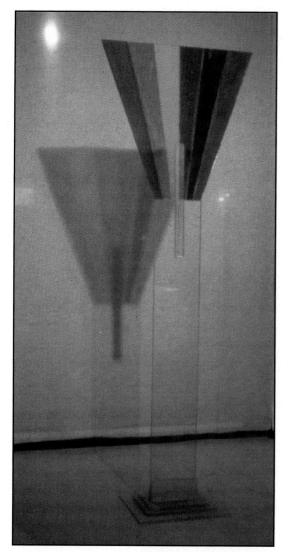

Lucartha Kohler, "Spectral Flag," 1992, 96" high x 24" wide x 10" diameter at base. (photo by the author)

"Spectral Flag" was made by dividing the glass triangle into six equal segments. Each color of the spectrum was fired separately, one at a time, as the fumes from individual colors don't like each other in the kiln. Greens and blues want to fire a few degrees higher than the reds and purples. Yellow and orange are pretty forgiving. They are also the least expensive.

The application of these liquid metals can be difficult. The surface of the glass object must be absolutely clean and free from dust, grease, fingerprints and moisture. The brush or applicator and the working environment must also be very clean. Any floating particles of dust in the atmosphere settling on the surface will show up when fired. The liquid must flow evenly when applied; thick or thin areas will be apparent especially on transparent glass. The surface of the glass object is an important factor contributing to the final result. If the metals are applied to a matte surface, when fired, they will appear dull. When they are fired on a highly-polished surface, they will appear shiny. Over-firing can also cause the metals to have a dull appearance or burn out altogether.

Firing Lusters

When firing lusters and metals, there are several unique considerations. They will assume the object's surface texture; a shiny surface will fire bright, a matte-surface will fire dull. The material must be absolutely dry. This takes at least six hours, preferably overnight. The most important factor is ventilation. The kiln should not be fully loaded and objects should not be placed too close together. The kiln should be turned on low, the lid propped open about 12" and peep holes should be left unplugged for the first hour or 500F. The lid can then be lowered to about 6" and the kiln turned to medium until all the smoke and odor have disappeared. Lusters like air circulation. The kiln lid can then be closed, still leaving the peep holes open until the appropriate temperature is obtained. Close the peep holes and allow the kiln to cool. When within annealing range, assume an appropriate annealing schedule.

Although all the techniques discussed thus far have had an applied design heritage, these techniques are not limited to remain within this fate. Artists today are meeting the creative challenges offered by old techniques, either as a revival of that technique or as a new direction and application of it. Glass is a material to create art; technical procedures are a way to create it.

Silvering

Silvering of glass is a term used to refer to the gilding of glass by chemical processes, most often used to create mirrors. Silver,

Charles Parriot, "Silver Hunter," 1994, blown glass, mirrored, mixed media, 24" x 18" x 10". (photo courtesy the artist, photo by Russell Johnson)

gold, copper, aluminum and tin as well as many other combinations may be used. The most common method of silvering glass involves the use of silver nitrate, stannous (tin) chloride and potassium hydroxide.

Commercially manufactured mirrors have been incorporated into the visual vocabulary of many contemporary artists. Charles Parriot has used commercial mirroring to his own end. The possibility of artists creating their own mirror surfaces exists and some information, though sparse, is available. It seems the old mirror craftsmen were as secretive as the old glassmakers. The chemicals necessary for silvering are available from Peacock Laboratory in concentrated form and should be diluted with distilled water and mixed together according to the manufacturer's directions.

The polished glass is prepared by scrubbing the surface with polishing compound and washing with distilled water, then coating with a solution of tin chloride and washing again with distilled water. The silver coating solution is then poured onto the wet plate and allowed to stand for 10 to 20 minutes. The residue remaining is then removed with a piece of wet leather and the glass is again washed. When dry, it is coated with mirror backing paint and varnished.

The coating process can be more effectively accomplished by spraying. The following is a list of the equipment needed to perform chemical spray silverings[2]:

Chemical spray silverings
1. Compressed air
2. Two-stage compressed air regulator
3. Air-hose with a tee coupling
4. One-nozzle air brush
5. Two-nozzle air brush
6. Four 1-liter aspirator bottles
7. Tygon tubing 0.625 cm inside diameter, 30.5 m
8. Four 25 ml graduated cylinders
9. 1000 ml graduated cylinder
10. Calcium carbonate, CP
11. Cleaning solution
12. Concentrated silvering chemicals: silver, activator, reducing and sensitizing solutions
13. Distilled water (several gallons)
14. Rubber gloves
15. Respirator
16. Air-hose with valve-type nozzle

Formula for diluting and mixing chemicals:
    15 ml silver solution plus 450 ml distilled water
    15 ml activator solution plus 450 ml distilled water, combine in bottle S
    15 ml reducer solution plus 450 ml distilled water, combine in bottle R
    15 ml sensitizer solution plus 450 ml distilled water, combine in bottle 93

A. Bottles S and R connect to the two nozzle gun.

B. Bottle 93 is connected to the one nozzle gun.

C. The fourth bottle is filled with distilled water.

D. Immediately before use, the chemicals should be warmed to 61C in a water bath.

E. The glass to be coated should be propped up to provide drainage and wrapped with a polyethelene sheet to minimize the mess

F. The mirror must be thoroughly cleaned (this is the most important step in a successful silvering). Start by scrubbing the surface with a polishing compound and a clean felt pad. Flush the surface with water. Wash the surface with cleaning solution. Rinse with distilled water. Wash again, with one teaspoon of calcium carbonate and again with distilled water. A third washing, again with the cleaning solution, and rinse with distilled water.

G. Using the single nozzle air brush, spray the entire surface with the sensitizer solution using broad sweeping strokes beginning at the top of the mirror and working downward. After 30 seconds, connect the distilled water in the fourth aspirator bottle to the single nozzle gun and rinse off the sensitizer. During all spraying operations, respirators should be worn, as the mist is irritating to the nose and throat.

H. Take up the dual nozzle air brush and begin spray silvering at the top of the mirror. The dual nozzle air brush is used to apply the silver solution and the reducing solution simultaneously. Hold the gun about 30 cm from the work and move slowly back and fourth across the surface until the bottom is reached. Repeat, working from top to bottom until desired thickness is obtained. Rinse the surface with distilled water and blow dry using an air hose.

I. The surface may have a dull appearance: to brighten the surface, a paste of red rouge mixed with methyl alcohol is rubbed over the coating. As the alcohol evaporates, the surface is wiped clean.

Colored mirrors can be produced either by silvering colored glass or by coating transparent glass with a colored-metal or metallic compound. Lead, gold and copper can be applied to polished plate glass in a manner similar to that of silvering, resulting in a tinted reflective metal coating. Gold mirrors are golden brown, copper mirrors are pink and lead mirrors are blue-gray. Included here are formulas for each process; for more detailed information refer to the article, "Colored Silvering of Glass" by Bruno Schweig.[3]

Solution for lead sulfide mirrors

Lead nitrate or acetate: 5%
Thiocarbamide: 1.6%
Sodium or potassium hydroxide: 0.6%
    The coating solution is mixed from equal parts of the three solutions. The coating is applied in the same manner as silver solutions. It might be necessary to coat a second or even a third time.

Solution for gold mirrors

Solution #1
3 grams gold chloride dissolved in 80 cc distilled water

Solution #2
8 grams sodium carbonate (crystals) dissolved in 80 cc distilled water

Solution #3
5 cc formaldehyde, diluted with 80 cc distilled water
    The coating solution is mixed from equal parts of the three solutions. The glass is cleaned, as for silvering, and coated with a solution of tin chloride (using a stronger concentration than usual) and washed again with distilled water. The gold solution is applied by pouring on the surface and allowed to stand about 20 minutes. As a rule, the thin gold film has to be protected by a layer of silver immediately after washing.

Solution for copper mirror

Solution #1
4 grams copper sulfate, dissolved in 1000 cc distilled water
15 grams rochelle salt
9 grams caustic soda

Solution #2
200 cc formaldehyde (solution #2 is added to solution #1)
    The glass is prepared as for silvering, then a thin transparent layer of silver is first deposited before coating with the copper solution. Colors varying from silver to reddish-pink can be obtained.

Safety precautions: It is wise when handling chemicals of any kind to be extra cautious. The work area should be kept separate from other work areas; clean and free from dust. It should be adequately ventilated–chemical fumes are as harmful as the liquid. Adequate protective clothing should be worn: definitely rubber gloves and a respirator. A proper disposal system for used chemicals should be incorporated, as hazardous chemicals are harmful to the environment. Before handling any chemical, it is wise to become aware of specific safety precautions, treatment and antidotes. Such information is available from the supplier along with instructions for handling.

Electroplating

Another means of obtaining a metal coating on a glass surface is by electroplating. Metals such as gold, silver, copper and chromium can be electroplated onto any glass surface, if it is properly prepared. The process is the electrodeposition of metal. Electric current is used to move positively charged metal particles through a solution and then deposit them on an object that has been given a negative charge. This is accomplished by placing the plating metal and the object to be plated in a chemical bath. The object is attached to the negative pole of a direct current source. The desired metal is attached to the positive pole. The metal ions flow from the positively charged metal through the solution to the negatively charged object; thus depositing a thin coating of metal on its surface.

As glass is non-metallic, it must be made electrically conductive to be plated. This may be accomplished in several ways. There are commercial conductive silver-based paints available from Acheson Colloids Co. and Safer Solutions (see "Supply Source" section). A deposit of fine metal powder can be applied by mixing the powder with a binder and sprayed or brushed on the area to be plated. The surface of the object to be plated can be lightly sand-blasted to better retain the metal coating.

Electroplating can be done commercially, or you can build your own equipment. For more information on the procedures and directions for assembling the equipment, read *Electroplating and Electroforming for Artists and Craftsmen*, Lee Scott Newman and Jay Hartley Newman.

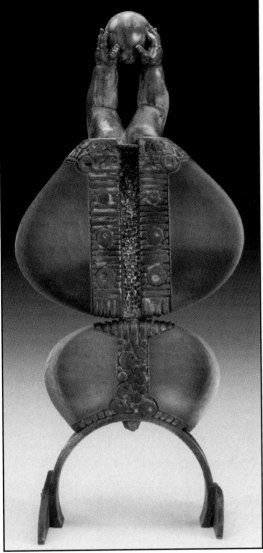

David Lewin, "Learning to Hold," 1996, 26-1/2" high x 12" wide x 7" diameter. (photo courtesy the artist)

David Lewin, "Learning to Hold."

There are a few artists currently working with electroplating. David Lewin combines electroplated glass and non-glass objects in his allegorical sculptures. In "Learning to Hold," the arms are plastic doll arms copper plated. Hopefully, many more artists will explore new directions and applications for electrodeposition of metal in connection with glass.

Vacuum Deposition

In addition to electrodeposition of metals, there is a process referred to as vacuum deposition. This process incorporates the use of a vacuum chamber, metallic iconel and quartz. The glass is placed in a vacuum chamber and a tungsten filament wired to an

Larry Bell, "The Iceberg and Its Shadow," 1974, 56 panels of 3/8" clear and gray plate glass coated with iconel and quartz, each panel 60" wide, heights vary from 57" to 100". (photo courtesy the artist)

electrical source is placed in close proximity to the glass. The filament, when charged, gets hot enough to change the material from a solid to a vapor. The vapor fills the chamber, depositing a thin metallic film on the glass. The film is permanent. Color is controlled by the amounts of iconel and quartz and by the position of the filament in relation to the glass.

Larry Bell is a pioneer in the exploration of industrial applications for use in artistic endeavors. He first employed industrial techniques to coat the glass surfaces of his minimal constructions. Unsatisfied by the limitations imposed by industrial equipment, he mastered the construction and use of equipment, enabling him to produce his monumental environmental works of art. The coating is deliberately controlled to manipulate light and, in so doing, controlling the optical experience of the viewer. Bell highly valued the process of his work, which is ultimately reflected in the work itself. The challenge of mastering the machine and the application of industrial techniques was a primary directing force for his work. The fact that he presents us with such profound visual experiences seems almost secondary to his purpose, or perhaps the two are so deeply entwined that we, the viewer, cannot distinguish the process from the experience.

Cutting and Engraving

Decorative engraving and cutting of glass had its origins during the Roman Empire, most likely coinciding with the origins of blown forms. "The Portland Vase" from the first century BC is an example of early cameo cutting. The earliest techniques were adapted from those of lapidary or gemstone workers. Wheels used for cutting were made of stone; sand was used as the abrasive and water as the coolant. The wheels were most likely turned by water or a simple treadle. To execute a cut design, the object is held against a coarse rotating wheel to rough out a design. Then a succession of finer wheels are used to refine the design. The final polishing is done with rottenstone and pumice on wheels made from a soft wood, cork or felt.

The development of a fine-quality lead crystal by George Ravenscroft in the late 17th century led to the English development of cut glass. By the 19th century, it had become the most popular form of decorating glass tableware. The glass was cut in V-shaped grooves and brought to a high polish, allowing the light to be reflected in a myriad of directions. Modern techniques are much the same; however, diamond-coated wheels and electricity speed-up the process.

Eric Hilton came to the United States from Scotland many years ago. It was there that he learned the traditional art of cutting and engraving. Some of those many years, he designed engraved works for Steuben, gaining an international reputation for his work in optical crystal. His own intricate assemblage of illusionistic puzzle pieces are made by first slumping optical crystal into molds to give each piece its unique shape. The pieces are then cut, polished, etched and

Eric Hilton, "Equinox," 1997, 11.5" high x 15.5" wide, nine units if glass, symbolic imagery of winter and spring engraved on three pyramids. (photo courtesy of the artist)

engraved by sandblasting into magical crystal-like structures where images are reflected over and over.

Wheel engraving is similar to cutting; a series of smaller wheels are used and the finish is usually left unpolished. Copper wheel engraving employs a series of soft copper wheels mounted on a shaft. The size of these wheels ranges from 1/16" up to 4" in diameter and vary in thickness from 0.64" to 0.25". The surfaces of the wheels can be round, flat or pointed. A fine abrasive such as silicon carbide or aluminum oxide mixed with kerosene and corn oil does the actual cutting. The finish is generally left unpolished. The most successful development of this type of engraving occurred in Germany, especially the region of Bavaria.

The art of stipple or hand-engraving developed as a result of the popularity of Venetian glass in Europe. The thinly-blown glass was not suitable for copper wheel engraving. Diamond tools were used

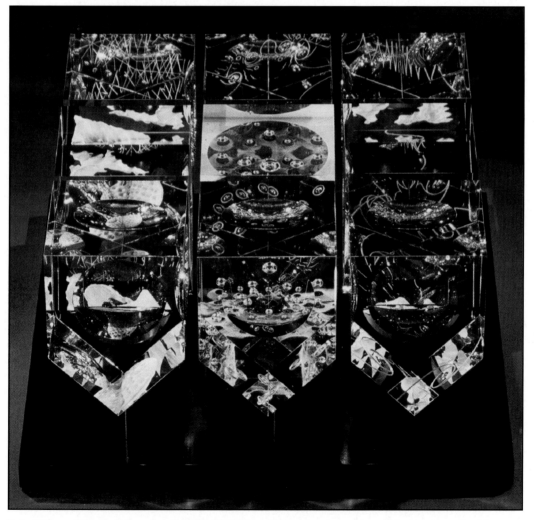

Eric Hilton, "Spell of Creation," 1995, 7" high x 15" wide, nine units of glass engraved with symbolic imagery. (photo courtesy of the artist)

113

to create fine delicate line drawings. During the 17th and 18th centuries, diamond-point engraving was developed to its height in the Netherlands.

Hand-engraving is done with a pencil-like carbide or diamond-tipped stylus. A modern version is a hand-held electric engraver with carbide or diamond tips. The technique of hand engraving involves a series of lines or stipples (dots) placed close together. Variety of line is achieved by pressure and space between the lines or dots. Diamond-impregnated wheels and tools are also used for cutting and engraving.

Acid Etching and Frosting

Etching, frosting and polishing by chemical corrosion is a far more recent industrial process. Acid etching is usually done with hydrofluoric acid, sometimes combined with other acids, depending on the type of glass. A design is masked out on the surface of the object and then placed in a bath of a dilute solution of acid. The acid attacks the silicates in the exposed areas, breaking them down to form silicon fluoride gas. The gas escapes, resulting in a corrosion of the surface; when the desired depth of corrosion is obtained, the acid is neutralized by water.

As hydrofluoric acid and the gases it forms are extremely hazardous, even in very dilute forms, utmost care need be taken to follow all recommended safety precautions. The process is not recommended, as hydrofluoric acid can be deadly. The problem is acid burns can go undetected. The acid does not burn the skin at first, but penetrates directly to the bone beneath where it begins to attack and dissolve bone. If untreated, it will continue to erode, causing bone loss. Inhalation of fumes can cause pulmonary edema. Ingestion can be fatal.

Abrasive Blasting and Carving

Engraving, cutting, acid frosting and etching techniques have all been replaced by abrasive blast techniques, especially in the artist's studio. The term "sand blasting" evolved as sand was the first abrasive material used for this process. Minute particles of abrasive material, mostly aluminum oxide or silicon carbide, are propelled through a nozzle, under pressure, fracturing the surface of glass in an overall pattern. An infinite variety of surface effects, including deep relief cuts, can be obtained with a sand-blaster, ranging from a general overall frosting on the surface of the glass to deep holes cut completely through the object. Delicate line drawings can be executed with the use of masking materials. By controlling the masking procedure, a variety of surface textures and depth-of-relief drawing can be obtained.

Masking materials can be simple masking tape or adhesive-backed vinyl films. More complex precut plastic or rubber stencils can be glued in place with a water soluble glue. Hot bee's wax can be painted on with a brush or stylus in the same manner it is applied to fabric in batik techniques. Photo-resist stencils can be made from a film positive, a laser printed vellum or transparent photo copy. Artwork is transferred onto a photo resist film or applied to an object via coating with a direct emulsion and exposing with ultraviolet light.

Barry Sautner has developed a sand carving technique that duplicates the intricate diatreta and cameo cutting of ancient Roman glass. He takes a cased blank of two or more layers and covers the entire piece with resist tape. The design is drawn onto the tape and the parts surrounding the design are cut away. These areas are sandblasted through to the first layer of glass revealing the background color. The remaining resist tape is removed, exposing a silhouette of his design. The design is then sand-carved with a pencil blaster with various tips as small as 0.003". The glass is sculpted into a bas-relief form and then undercut around the edges to give a more three-dimensional effect.

If you are doing any type of cutting, you will need a

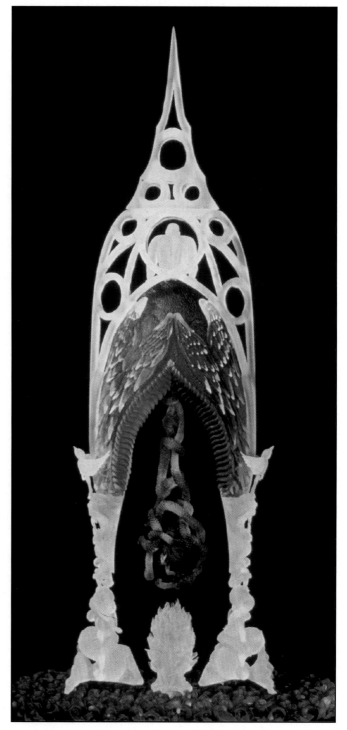

Barry Sautner, "The Seventh Day," 1993, 18-1/8" high x 9-1/8" wide x 4" deep. (photo courtesy of the artist)

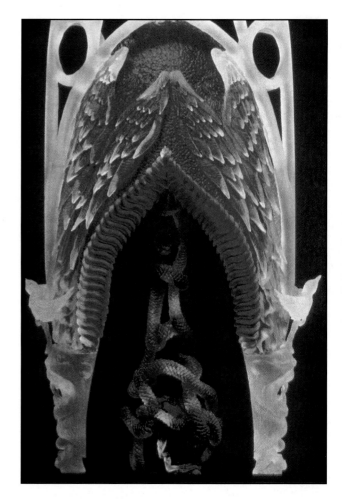

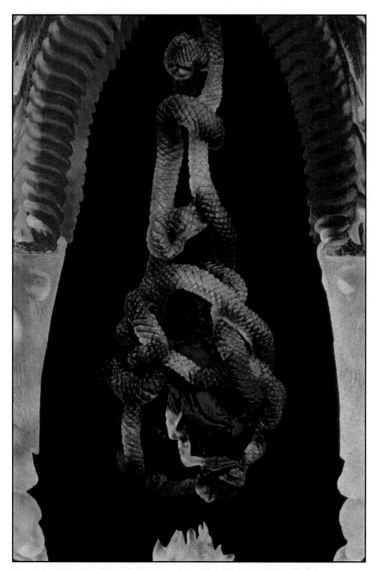

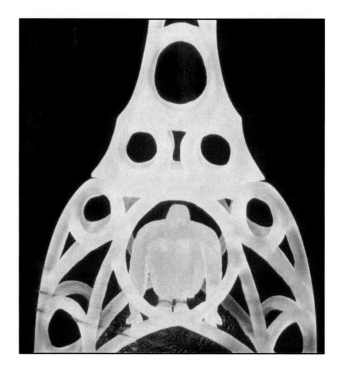

Various views of Barry Sautner's, "The Seventh Day."
(photos courtesy of the artist)

Front view of Barry Sautner's "The Struggle," 1989, 7-1/2" x 3" diameter. (photo courtesy of the artist)

Back view of Barry Sautner's "The Struggle."

compressor capable of delivering 125 pounds-per-square-inch of pressure (PSI) and a gun sturdy enough to deliver the abrasive at 25 CFM. The nozzle will need to be replaced occasionally, as the abrasive action wears out the lining of the orifice. The size nozzle will determine the breadth of spray you need; there is a variety of nozzle sizes, including abrasive air brushes. The area around the intended cut must be masked with a heavy duty masking material. The amount of pressure and the length of time it takes to cut through the material depends on the PSI and the type of system. Ideally, a pressure pot is better than a siphon system for deep cuts and carving.

Jutta Cuny-Franz, an Austrian artist whose life was cut short by a tragic accident in 1983, used a sandblaster as one would use a chisel to carve away material in a traditional sculpture sense. She used the nozzle of a sandblaster to carve deep into the body of thick glass plates. Many sheets were stacked and assembled, then negative shapes were carved into them with jets of sand. "The glass sheets were piled one over the other and assembled to form cubes or columns of various sizes, destined to contain negative, that means hollow sculptures, shaped with sandblast and visible to the viewer as virtual positive forms. Visible, but untouchable and because of the complex game of reflexes unseizable in their true reality," from statement written by her on April 5, 1982.

Dr. Helmut Ricke, director of the Kunst Museum in Dusseldorf, Germany, and

Jutta Cuny Franz, "Grand Affrontement Penetration," 1979, 2 x 40 cm x 40 cm x 40 cm, glass and polyester. (photos courtesy of Jutta Cuny Franz Foundation, photo by Enrico Cattaneo)

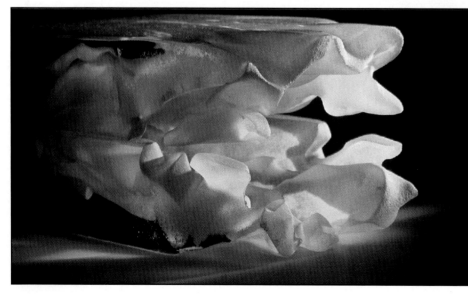

Jutta Cuny Franz, "Grand Affrontement Penetration" close-up.

editor of Neus/Glas-New Glass, says of Jutta Cuny-Franz, "She came from sculpture, that is, from problems of sculptural and formal expression, to glass as the material most suited to her conceptions...The artist chooses the material that he feels drawn to."[4]

Gilding

The gilding of glass or gold leafing is an ancient process whose modern application has been for the most part relegated to window signage. There are several procedures for gilding glass, depending on the type of surface. The most common one for window glass involves a gelatin water size. This process works well when the gilding is to be viewed through transparent glass from the reverse side. Tack gilding with varnish or paint works best on matte surfaces or sculptural objects with texture.

The most important factor for successful gilding is the cleanliness of the glass surface. Any oil, finger prints or cleanser residue will cause incomplete bonding of the leaf. Isopropyl alcohol regent grade is the best cleanser. New plate glass may need to be cleaned with a mild abrasive cleanser first to create a surface for the size to adhere.

Jutta Cuny Franz with sandblaster. (photo courtesy of Jutta Cuny Franz Foundation, photo by Enrico Cattaneo)

Gold, silver, palladium and copper leaf is available in books of 25 leaves measuring 3-3/8" x 3-3/4". Tools include a camel hair gilding tip which measures about 3-1/2" wide by 2-3/4" long, a camel hair water size brush 2" wide and cotton batting. The tools, gelatin, varnishes and books of leaves can be purchased from most art supply stores or gilding suppliers.

To make 1 pint of gelatin water size, put two empty #00 gelatin capsules from a pharmacist or six to eight diamonds of sheet gelatin in a pan with a 1/2 cup of distilled water, soak for 30 minutes and then heat gently, do not boil, until gelatin is dissolved. Add the remaining amount of water. If there are any lumps or undissolved gelatin, the mixture must be sieved through a fine-mesh screen. Use the water size right away as it will thicken and become lumpy.

To gild, get plenty of water size on the brush and flow on to the surface to be gilded. Make sure there is plenty of size on the glass, as each leaf will float on the surface and be a bit wrinkled at first. With enough size, it will straighten out. If the size is too thin, it will remain wrinkled. Cover an area large enough to apply a few leaves at a time. To pick up each leaf from the book, charge the gilding tip by passing it lightly over your hair to pick up a small amount of oil. Place the bristles of the tip about half-way onto the sheet. Carefully lift off and bring the leaf to the glass and, with a snapping motion, place it in position. This will take some practice. When the gild is dry, remove the wrinkles by rubbing over the surface with cotton. Second or third layers can be added at this time, either solid or as patches to fill imperfections. A back-up coating of clear varnish will protect the gilding.

Gold size is a special varnish that is used to tack gild. This procedure works best on non-glassy or texture surfaces. Leaf is applied in the same manner as water size to a paint or varnish that is not yet dry, but tacky. It's possible to use any kind of paint or varnish; however, it should be free of brush marks, as they will show through the leaf. For more detailed information, see *Gold Leaf Techniques* by Kent H. Smith, Signs of the Times Publishing Co., Cincinnati.

Reverse Painting on Glass

The earliest reverse glass paintings were probably done in Venice during the 13th century. The first Venetian works on glass were made by drawing through gold leaf attached to the glass with glue. The Venetians called this work "sgraffito" from the Italian word "scratch." This technique dates back to early Roman times; gold-decorated bowls were found from the first century BC. The gold engravings from the 13th century resemble the ancient ones and were most likely influenced by them. The artists of that time did gold engraving with painted backgrounds on the backs of religious medallions. This engraving technique is the first evidence of drawing and painting in reverse. As time passed, more paint was added; by the 16th century, they were mostly paint.

Reverse painting is done on the backside of a glass surface. The image is reversed when the work is complete. The layers of paint must be built up from the front as you view the painting through the glass–totally reverse thinking. A master of that complex process is Judy Jensen. Her narrative glass canvases recall motifs from medieval paintings filled with archetypal symbols. Trompe L'oeil images and painterly illustrations play with suggestive ideas from many cultures, as well as her own personal experience. She refers to these paintings as "collages of memories and meanings, edited together with glass and paint."

Judy Jensen, "Crusading," 1995, 44" high x 26.5" wide, reverse painting on glass. (photo courtesy the artist, photo by Emil Vogely)

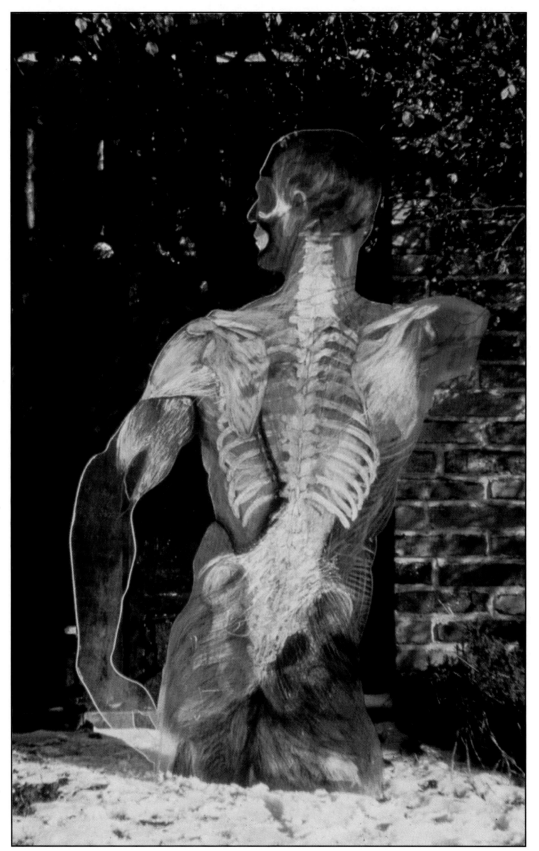

*Dana Zamechnikova, "Bony Man," 1996, painted glass, 185 cm x 135 cm x 1.6 cm.
(photo courtesy the artist)*

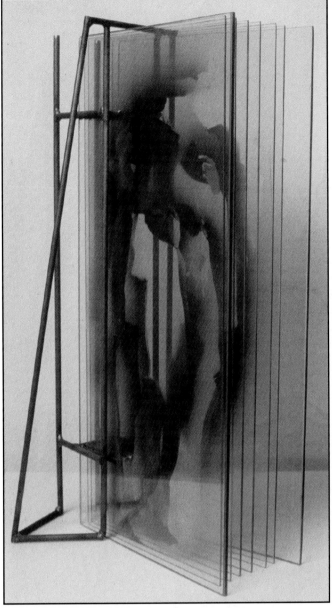

Suzanne Reese Horvitz, "Self Portrait Glass Book," 1991 steel glass, Plexiglas, 26" high x 18" wide x 6" deep. (photo courtesy of the artist)

Suzanne Reese Horvitz, "Glass Book," 1990, painted glass and steel, 50" high x 40" wide x 12" deep. (photo courtesy of the artist)

Sue Horvitz is another artist using glass as a canvas. Best known as a book artist, her work includes the use of gilding with gold and silver combined with paints. Text is an important part of her visual vocabulary. She uses the panes of glass as transparent pages to tell mysterious and suggestive stories.

Suzanne Reese Horvitz, "Golden Tears," 1991, painted glass, gold leaf and steel, 50" high x 40" wide x 12" deep. (photo courtesy of the artist)

Carol Cohen uses layers of transparent glass and paint to construct a visual picture that is made up of individual parts, which, when viewed, optically contribute to a whole image.

Carol Cohen, "Black Scribble Cow," 1987, stacked and painted glass, 5" high x 12" wide x 8" deep. (photo courtesy of the artist)

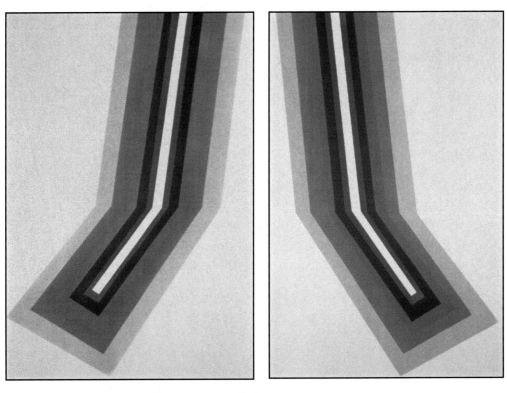

Harvey K. Littleton, "Refraction" 36" high x 24" wide, Diptych 1994, Vitreograph, (photos courtesy Littleton Co. Inc.)

Printmaking

Printmaking techniques, although two-dimensional in character, can be incorporated into three-dimensional sculptural forms. Most printmaking techniques can be applied to glass. Except for silk-screen techniques, very few artists have explored the use of glass as a printable surface. If the glass surface is to be rendered dishwasher safe, the pigment used must be firable ceramic colors such as glass enamels or paints. Sign painters' enamels and epoxy paints, although not permanently bonded to the glass can be quite durable.

Vitreograph press. Littleton Studios. (photo courtesy Littleton Co. Inc.)

Vitreograph press. Littleton Studios. (photo courtesy Littleton Co. Inc.)

As glass is resilient, it will withstand an enormous amount of pressure evenly applied. A glass plate can be used as a printing plate or as a surface to be printed on. Harvey Littleton developed a technique of using float glass as a printing plate based on book illustrations made from glass plates in Vienna during the 1840s. In some cases, this process is more successful than traditional printing techniques.

Photographic images can be silk-screened on to a glass surface, as well as the glass itself, becoming a photographic negative or positive. Some of the earliest photographic negatives were made from a colliden-coated glass plate. Industry has used lithography for bottle labeling since the early 1900s. The first use of printing on bottles was done with decals. The image was first printed on paper-coated with glue, then transferred to the glass bottle and fired. More recent advances in specialized machines involve the printing process with the forming process. The bottle is printed with a silk screen on the assembly line

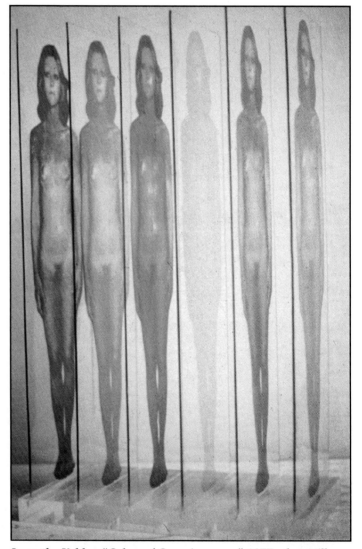

Lucartha Kohler, "Herstory," 1995, cast glass, photo silk-screen, fired enamels.

Lucartha Kohler, "Colors of Consciousness," 1977, photo silk-screen, fired enamels. (photo courtesy of the Corning Museum)

between the forming machine and the lehr.

In my own work, I have used the photo silk-screen technique developed for industrial applications. I saw in the technique the ability to transfer figurative images to transparent glass and to layer these images to create metaphorical statements. In "Colors of Consciousness," a single figure was printed in a succession of colors stating the nature of metaphysical reality as it is expressed by our intuitive knowledge.

This is an area virtually untapped for creative expression. There are very few artists working with photographic or printmaking techniques; either as an end, or as a means to an end. It is my hope that many more artists will see the possibilities of these techniques and will explore the challenges available. There are even greater challenges in areas such as xerography and holography. The technical information is sparse, but obtainable for a brave pioneer.

Silk-Screen

It is possible to use traditional silk-screen techniques to print on glass. The silk-screen, or screens in a multi-colored print, are used in the same manner as ordinary silk screen printing on a paper surface. Again, if the glass is to be permanent, enamels or glass colors must be used as the pigment and fired.

There are several considerations when printing with large areas of a single color, because light passes through glass, any imperfections in the deposition of the pigment will show when fired. It is advisable to first screen the pigment through a fine screen (300 mesh) and then print with a coarse screen (200 mesh).

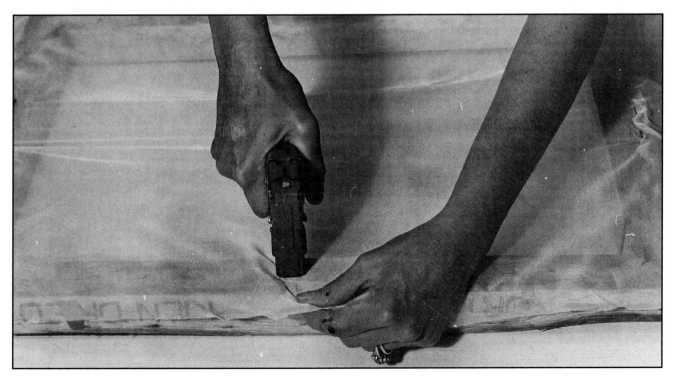

Stretching fabric for silk-screen.

The following is a way to make a silk screen:

1. To construct a silk-screen you will need 2″ x 2″ lumber. Allow at least 2″ to 4″ around the edges of your image to facilitate printing.

2. Cut your lumber to the desired length, allowing for mitered corners.

3. Assemble the frame; I found half-inch staples and glue adequate, except for very large frames.

4. Cut the fabric slightly larger than the frame dimensions. Beginning in the center of one side, staple the fabric to the frame. Pull the fabric taut to the opposite side and staple. Pull the third side taut, but keep the grain of the fabric in view, staple. Pull taut again to the opposite side of the frame and staple again. Work evenly around the frame; stapling from the center of each side until you reach the corners. It is very important to have the screen stretched tight.

5. Next, cover all exposed wood with plastic coated (duct) tape.

6. Clean the screen to remove any finish or grease remaining on the fabric. Allow the screen to dry thoroughly.

There are several ways to prepare a stencil for silk-screen printing. For a hand-cut stencil, you begin with a master drawing; if multicolored, a separate stencil must be cut and a separate screen prepared for each color. There are commercial stencil films available, but a simple tracing paper stencil can be applied to the screen with tuche or glue. The film or tracing paper is laid over the master drawing and cut with a stencil-cutting knife, scalpel or razor-blade.

Place the cut stencil on a flat clean surface, positive image facing up. If tracing paper is used, a thin coat of glue will need to be applied. For commercial film, follow the manufacturer's directions. Place the screen on top of the stencil and apply pressure to stick the stencil to the screen. An alternative method is a liquid screen filler or block out. Place the screen over your master drawing and, with a paint brush, block out all areas except the ones to be printed. A third alternative to silk-screen preparation is the photo silk-screen process. Once the stencil or photo image is applied to the screen, you are ready to print.

Photo Silk-Screen Printing

The early development of photography shared in the development of the photo silk-screen technique on glass. In the 1830s, the French inventor Louis J.M. Daquerre produced the first popular form of photography. With a camera, he exposed a light-sensitive metal plate, developed the image with mercury vapor and fixed it with common salt. These early photographs were called daquerreo-types. In 1852, the British scientist William Henry Fox Talbot, patented a process for making a photographic etching on a steel plate using potassium bichromate and gelatin. In 1851, Frederick Scott Archer, British photographer introduced still another new process. A glass plate was coated with a wet, sticky substance called colliden, then dipped in light-sensitive silver salts.

Recent technical advancements in photography, as well as photographic processes, have made photo silk-screen techniques accessible to the artist working in glass. There are many ways to approach the silk-screen process and there are alternative photographic processes that do not require the use of a silk-screen.

Film Positive

The first step and most critical, is the positive halftone film. This halftone film separates the photo image into dots. The density of the dots produce shades from white through to gray and black. The size of the screen (dots per line) must correspond with the size mesh screen you are using. A 65-line halftone screen will correspond with 200 mesh dacron or 20xx silk. If you do not have experience in the darkroom, I suggest that you enlist the help of one who does; or have someone do this step for you. Any silk-screen supply company or printing house has the equipment.

To begin, you will need a dark room, enlarger, 65-line halftone screen, Kodak Ortho film type 3, sheet of clear glass, fine line developer, stop bath and fixer.

1. Under safelight conditions, focus your negative on a scrap of paper to determine the size of the image, just as you would for printing photographic paper.
2. When ready, place your sheet of Ortho film, emulsion side up (gray) under your enlarger and lay your halftone screen on top, then add your piece of clear glass.
3. Expose (exposure time varies with density of negative, F-stop setting and distance). An approximate time for an 8" by 10" image at F8 could be 17 seconds. As in all photographic work, it is advisable to make test exposures.
4. Develop with a gentle agitation until the darkest areas are black. This should take about two minutes.
5. Place your film in stop bath, then fixer. The length of time to fix will be determined by the type of fixer you're using. When fixed properly, all white areas should be clear.
6. Wash film to remove excess silver salts; approximately 20 minutes then hang to dry.
7. You will need to construct a silk-screen: 200-mesh dacron or nylon or 20xx silk is recommended to match the 65-line halftone screen.
8. Clean the screen and allow to dry thoroughly. There are two methods of applying the image to a silk-screen; direct screen emulsion is a coating applied directly to the screen. The indirect method involves the use of a light-sensitive film applied to the silk-screen.

Direct Screen Emulsion

I use Ulano direct screen emulsion 569; however, there are many similar products available from silk-screen suppliers. Ulano 569 is a diazo-based emulsion, easy to handle, has a long shelf life and is easily removed from your screen. When choosing an emulsion, be sure it is compatible with the pigments and binders you're using. The removal of some emulsions can be difficult; soaking for days in Clorox may destroy the fabric.

To coat the screen:

1. Mix the emulsion and the sensitizer according to package directions.
2. Under safelight, stand the screen upright and squeegee a thin, even coat of emulsion on the outside surface.
3. Turn and squeegee the inside surface. Make sure the coating is even. Thick areas will not expose the same as thin areas–it may take some practice.
4. Dry thoroughly and store the screen in black plastic (trash) bags until you're ready to use it, as ambient light will expose the screen.
5. To expose the image on the screen, you will need a light source. Here is the one I use (there are many sources much better, but this was most economically feasible): I began with a box construction 20" by 30" long and 10" deep. On the inside surfaces of the box, I glued aluminum foil. I purchased four separate 15 watt fluorescent tubes and wired them together; then attached them to the floor of the box. I drilled a hole in the top for the electrical wire and 1" holes on the sides for ventilation. To finish the box, I placed a 3/16" thick sheet of glass on top.

Light box, 20" x 30" x 10".

Test First

Before you begin, it is advisable to make a step wedge test before you begin to expose your screen. To do this, coat a small screen, when dry, under safelight, place your film positive on the glass lid of the light box. Cut a strip of black paper and slip it under the film. Place your screen on top of the film and cover it with black paper and a piece of glass. Begin your exposure time at half the recommended time and gradually remove the paper strip in two- or three-minute intervals until five minutes beyond the recommended exposure time. Wash the screen and test print. Somewhere in that range, you should find the correct exposure time for your film density screen coating and light box.

When this is determined, you may proceed with your screen. Still under safelight, place your film positive on the lid of the light box, emulsion side up. Cover with the coated screen, emulsion side down. Place a piece of glass over this and cover with a piece of heavy black paper. To ensure good contact, I add weights; anything heavy, some old bricks work fine. Expose. Here are some estimated exposure times: Ulano 569 lightbox–8-10 minutes; carbon arc lamp–3-5 minutes; No. 2 photoflood, 15" above screen–3-4 minutes.

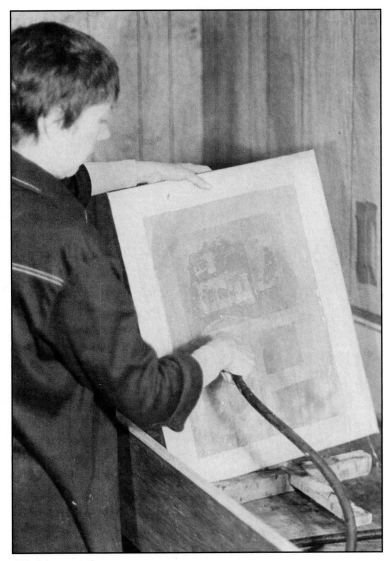

Washing out the screen.

To wash out the screen, use a hose with a spray attachment. Gently spray both sides with warm water until the image opens up; continue until all loose emulsion is removed. Stand screen on end to dry, a small fan will speed this along. To touch up and block out unwanted areas, use a screen filler or screen block out.

When you're finished printing your screen, you can remove the image with stencil remover liquid or Clorox. Do not use Clorox on silk, as it will deteriorate the fibers.

Indirect Method: Ulano Blue Poly

You will need a film positive. The image is exposed on the Blue Poly film, developed and them applied to the silk-screen. The screen is prepared the same as the direct screen method, making sure it is clean and free of grease. Work under safelight to transfer the film image.

1. Place the positive on the glass surface of the light box. Then put the Blue Poly film shiny side down. Always expose through the polyester support.
2. On top of the film; place a piece of glass and a black piece of paper on top of this. Make sure you have good contact. Exposure time will vary. To determine the best time with your light source, a step wedge test is recommended. Some approximate exposure times: light box–15 minutes; carbon arc light–3 minutes at 30"; photoflood light–20 minutes at 24".
3. To develop: mix the A/B developer according to package directions, develop the Blue Poly for 90 seconds.
4. Wash gently in warm water until all of the unexposed blue areas wash out. Finish the wash out by slowly cooling the water temperature to room temperature.
5. Place film, emulsion side up, on a flat surface covered with newsprint. Carefully lay the screen on top of the film. Excess moisture is removed by gently blotting with newsprint or paper towels. Allow to dry thoroughly. When dry, the plastic support may be gently peeled off. Screen is now ready to print or you may wish to block out unwanted areas using a screen filler.
6. To remove the image from the screen, simply wash in warm water. Do not use a water-base pigment with Blue Poly.

Direct Emulsion

For this type of emulsion, a photographic enlarger may be used. The screen is positioned like photographic paper under the enlarger; for larger screens, positioned horizontally. A color slide transparency may be used, or a film positive may be made by contact printing a black and white negative on ortho film. You do not need the halftone screen for this.

Under safelight conditions, a thin coat of emulsion is squeegeed onto the surface of the screen and allowed to dry. The screen is then exposed; check recommended exposure time on the package. After sponging the developer onto the screen (supplied with the emulsion) the screen is washed out under hot water. This can be done under room light. The unexposed portions of the screen dissolve in water, while the light-hardened portions remain.

The same type of emulsion can be used to directly coat an object or piece of glass. A negative film can be projected on to the glass with a slide projector or contact printed and exposed. The same type of direct emulsion used for the photo resist sand blast process can be used for the process.

Choice of Glass

The type of glass you use will be determined by the effect you wish to achieve. If you choose to begin with colored glass (and if a clear photo image is important), I recommend a flat smooth surface. The best types of stained glass are European antique, drawn antique and semi-antique. I would suggest test firing a small piece first as some colors tend to change in firing. You can also color your own glass by using an airbrush and the screening pigment thinned with water or a solvent. Single strength window glass, as well as plate glass, can be used successfully. Whichever glass you choose, be very careful that it is clean and free from dirt, grease and fingerprints. In my own work, I often use old window glass, because part of the mystical process of creating art is transforming an object from one existence to another.

There is a variety of commercial glass paints available. Glass enamels, china paints and high-fire enamels, such as Paradise Paints, all require firing. Many other types of paints can be used. Most direct screen emulsions are fine to use with water-base

Mixing pigment.

paints; the indirect film method, such as Blue Poly, must be used with oil-based paints. A binder, such as Reusche's squeegee medium or boiled linseed oil, is mixed with powdered enamels to be fired, or premixed oil base printing inks can be used.

To mix the pigment with the binder, use a flexible painting knife. An approximate proportion would be four-parts pigment to one-part medium. Mix thoroughly until a smooth, slightly thick consistency has been obtained. A small roller or brayer will roll out the pigment to remove any lumps that may clog your screen.

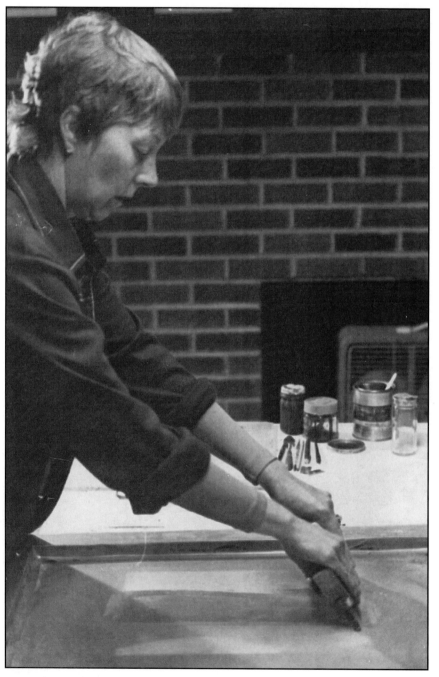

To print, lay your clean piece of glass on a flat surface. When your screen is in position, place a small amount of pigment across the top of your printing surface. With a firm, steady motion, squeegee (pull) the pigment across the screen. One or two passes should be sufficient. Allow to dry. If you want to print several colors, I recommend firing each color separately.

It is possible to make a four-color print. I recommend having color separation film positives made by a professional. A separate silk-screen is required for each color and registration keys are needed to align the images for printing. Reusche recommends the following enamels for color separation: 27-778 Blue, L-349 Amber 22-891 Carmine and 2840 Black. (To fire, refer to "Firing Enamels.")

Screening image.

Photography on Glass

Photographic images can be permanently applied to most glass surfaces. There are many approaches and techniques in addition to the silk-screen method. Many processes, from non-silver photography, printmaking and etching techniques, can be adapted for glass. To render permanent (or dishwasher safe), low-fire glass enamels need to be used as the pigment; then fired in a kiln to the appropriate temperature. Some direct photo-emulsions that are designed for silk-screen application or sandblast-resists can be mixed with powered glass enamels, then applied directly on a glass surface and exposed according to each manufacturers recommendations. Exposure can be a contact print through a film-positive or through a projected slide (this requires much longer exposure times). Experimentation is necessary as there is not a product designed to do the job. The few that existed in the past are no longer produced.

It is possible to make your own dichromate/colloid emulsion formula suitable for glass. A colloid is an organic substance like egg white, gelatin, sugar or gum arabic. When mixed with potassium dichromate, it becomes light sensitive. Areas exposed to ultraviolet light are hardened and set and become insoluble. The unexposed areas can be washed away with water.

Part A: 50% colloid solution

Part B: 50% dichromate solution (one-part ammonium dichromate to five-parts water)

Dry pigment can be added to this mixture. If powdered glass or glass enamels are added, the hardened gum binder burns off in the firing process, leaving behind the positive image.

Since the emulsion is light sensitive, coating and handling must take part in subdued or safelight conditions. The object to be coated must be clean and free from grease or oil. The mixture is brushed on with a wide soft bristle brush, then allowed to dry, then coated again and allowed to dry. A hair dryer can speed up the process. A film positive is placed over the coated surface and a sheet of clear glass or acrylic is placed over the film and exposed to UV light. Tests need to be done to determine accurate exposure times for your emulsion (see the silk-screen section for step-wedge exposure test).

Bonnie Biggs uses many non-fired photographic processes such as gel lifts, solvent transfers, photo emulsions, photo embossing and engraving in her work, as well as ink-wash drawings laminated between layers of glass. The photographic images are placed on the outside surfaces and serve to integrate the ink-wash drawings in the completed object.

Bonnie Biggs preparing layers of glass for lamination.

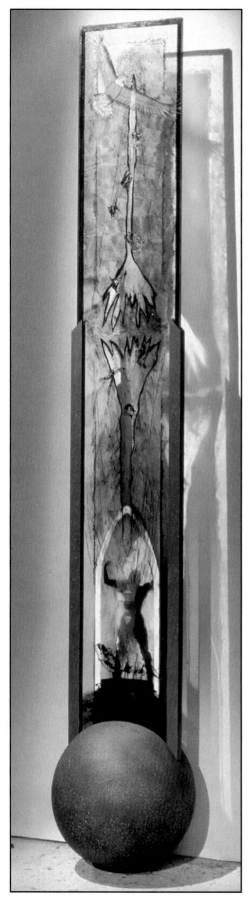

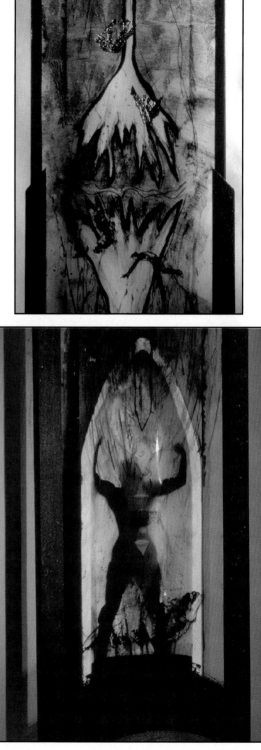

Bonnie Biggs, "Electro-Magnetic Flux," laminated glass with layered wash drawings, embossed photo images, photo emulsions, light, painted wood, 1997, 108" high x 18" wide x 18" deep. (photo courtesy of the artist)

Two photos above: Detail of Bonnie Biggs "Electro-Magnetic Flux." (photo courtesy of the artist)

Bonnie Biggs, "Street Fight," The Cure, Detail, photo emulsions, glass, ink, wood, 1996, 24" high x 8" wide x 2" deep. (photo courtesy of the artist)

Bonnie Biggs, "Thinking You," laminated glass with layered wash drawings, embossed photo images, painted wood, 1997, 24" high x 12" wide x 2.5" deep. (photo courtesy of the artist)

Xerography

There are several possible ways of using xerography (electrostatic photography) on glass. These techniques have been developed for industrial use; however, an inventive and creative approach by artists can transform most industrial techniques to studio applications.

The photographic aspects of xerography involve the formation of an electrostatic image on a layer of photoconductive material and the development of the image with finely divided powders.

As the standard xerographic powders used for reproduction on paper will not be permanent on glass, substitutions have to be made. Xerography developers consist of two components: carrier particles and powders. To formulate xerographic developers using ceramic colors, it is necessary to control the electrostatic charge between the carrier particles and the powder particles. The ceramic colors are used as the powder. The formulation of the proper developer is determined by the relationship of the powder and carrier material in the tribo-electric series. (The electrification of the powder and carrier is caused by magnetic attraction.) Once a carrier is determined, the two components may be mixed together to form a developer.

To transfer the powder from xerographic plate to glass, there must be good contact between the plate and the glass. To transfer an image to a glass surface, it is necessary to use a flexible plate or an intermediate transfer medium. To use an intermediate transfer medium, the powder image is first transferred to a paper or plastic sheet, the sheet with powder image is then placed in contact with the glass and the image transferred electrostatically. The ceramic powder developer can also be transferred to special decal paper and fixed with a protective coating.

At present, only one color can be fired at a time, additional colors can be printed in subsequent printings and superimposed. Either firing each color separately or at least allowing each color to dry thoroughly.

If permanence is not a factor in transferring an image to glass, there are several ways of incorporating a Xerox image printed with the standard xerographic powders. Standard xerographic powders consist of low-fusing temperature resins.

Heat transfer paper is probably the easiest way. You may be familiar with the iron-on tee-shirt transfer technique. To transfer the image onto a glass surface, you will need a source of heat and pressure. An iron may be used carefully. Heat must be introduced slowly and carefully. Using a hot iron on the glass surface will cause it to crack. I recommend placing several sheets of paper over the glass and transfer and gently iron the total surface of the glass, slowly increasing the temperature until the resin fuses.

There is also a transparent acetate for use in both black-and-white and color copiers. These transparencies may be used directly mounted with adhesive on the surface of the glass or they may by used as film positive for the photo silk-screen process. The design of the image can include photographs, drawings, paintings, found objects, printing, collage and montage. All of the preparatory work is done before the copy process. The process is simple: copy the art.

Finding the machine and the right paper is a little more difficult. Not all copy services stock the heat-transfer paper and the transparent acetate. Most major cities have copy services with color machines and can tell you where to locate the special papers.

For more information on the possibilities of electrostatic photography refer to *Copyart*, the first complete guide to the copy machine, by Patrick Firpo, Lester Alexander and Claudia Katayanagi, Richard Marek Publishers, NY; or *Alternative Photographic Processes* by Kent E Wade, Morgan and Morgan, NY.

Martha Madigan, "Elements," digital images on Star-phire glass, 1996, 28 feet high x 33 feet deep, each panel is 9 feet x 4 feet, First Union Center in Philadelphia. (photo courtesy of Michael Rosenfeld Gallery)

Detail of Martha Madigan's "Elements." (photo courtesy of Michael Rosenfeld Gallery)

Computer-Generated Photographic Images

Martha Madigan, a photographer, has used digital computer technology, photography and glass to create a suspended spiral sculpture for the First Union Sports and Entertainment Center in Philadelphia. The glass panels within the steel spiral contain silhouettes of athletes and performers superimposed on landscapes using images of elements in nature that correspond to the four ancient elements: air, fire, water and earth. The colorful digital images are laminated between two sheets of crystal-clear tempered glass, 3/8" thick. Each trapezoidal glass panels spiral 28 feet through the air. Each panel measures 4 feet wide x 6-1/2 feet on the shorter vertical side and 9 feet on the longer side.

References

1. Lenchner, Theodore, "Glass Decorator's Palette and Its Preparation," *Decorating in the Glass Industry*, Chapter 2, pp. 5-6, Dr. Alexis G. Pincus, Shung Huei Chang.
2. Armstrong, Bruce, "Chemical Spray Silverings," *Applied Optics*, Vol. 16, No. 11, November 1977, pp. 2785-2787.
3. Schweig, Bruno, "Colored Silvering of Glass," *Secondary Manufacturing in the Glass Industry*, Dr. Alexis G Pincus and S.H. Chang, Chapter 44, pp. 177-180.
4. Cuny-Franz, Jutta, Magic Glass, Jutta Cuny-Franz Foundation, Dr. Ruth-Maria Franz, 1990.

Section 7

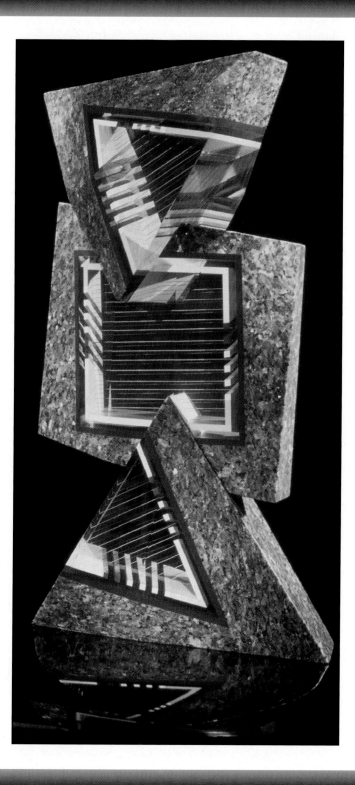

Cold Working

Glass has been cut and polished almost as long as it has been formed. Lapidary techniques were known to most ancient peoples. The techniques are simple. The difficulty lies in the tediousness of the task. A vivid description of the polishing of plate glass in the 17th century is found recorded by a Dr. Martin Lister in his journal, "A Journey to Paris in the Year 1698":[1]

"There they are polished: which employs daily 600 Men, and they hope in a little time to employ a 1000 in several galleries. In the lower they grind the course glass with a sand stone, the very same they pave the streets in Paris: of which broken they have great heaps in the courts of the work-houses: This stone is beat to powder, then sifted through a fine tamis. In the upper gallery, where they polish and give the last hand, they work in 3 rowes and 2 men at a plate, with ruddle and powdered haematites in water.

Dan Dailey, "Beaujolais," 1984, 15" x 26", vitrolite, blown glass, gold-plated brass, aluminum frame.

"The glasses are set fast in white puttie, upon flat tables of stone, sawed thin for that purpose. The grinding the edges and borders is very troublesome and odious for the horrid grating noise it makes, and which cannot be endured to one that is not used to it; and yet by long custom these fellows are so easie with it, they discourse together as nothing were. This is done below and out of the way of the rest."

Fortunately today, this process is not quite so laborious or noisy. The old-fashioned way still works, but with new high-tech diamond equipment, large pieces of glass can be polished in a fraction of the time. There are many exciting challenges available to artists and new forms of visual expression by cutting, carving, polishing and assembling pre-formed glass. Sheet glass, solid cast blocks, cast sculptural forms and hollow-blown forms can all be cut, carved, polished and assembled. Historically, glass was cut and polished for decorative ware, window glazing or looking glasses; today, the artist's imagination is free to establish new techniques and reuses of old techniques.

In this age of machine technology, the process is often as important as the art object being created. The deafening roar of machines can be extremely hazardous, yet an artist approaches this sense of danger as mountain climbers or race car drivers accept their particular challenge. The materials used are equally hazardous. Serious debilitating, even fatal, diseases can result from prolonged exposure to chemicals and abrasives. Fortunately, the awareness of health and safety hazards has greatly increased. Most hazardous or toxic material makers are required inform the consumer of the potential dangers and recommend proper safety precautions.

Dan Dailey is a skillful craftsman and artistic designer of objects made from glass. He uses all types of glass and all manner of forming

Dan Dailey, "Lizard," 1995, 9" high x 27" wide x 10" deep, black and green vitrolite, gold-plated bronze, orange bug.

143

methods to make his often whimsical and humorous works of art. He combines blown glass elements with shapes cut out of vitrolite and industrial plate glass. The forms are cut, polished and assembled using fabricated metal hardware.

William Carlson combines various colors and types of plate glass and granite into his asymmetrical constructions. Glass is first cut into small pieces, ground and polished and bonded together into larger sections. These are cut, ground and polished and combined with other types of glass and granite, then assembled into the final configurations.

Since the onset of the Industrial Revolution, machines to speed up all manner of physical labor have been designed and redesigned at an accelerated pace of invention. With today's vast range of industrial-quality tools

William Carlson, "Pragnanz Series," 33" high x 18" wide x 10", 1993, diameter, glass and granite. (photo courtesy of the artist)

William Carlson, "Vetro Muralis," 1996, 22-1/2" high x 19-1/2" wide, glass and granite. (photo courtesy of the artist, photo by Doug Schiable)

and equipment designed specifically for glass, you can cut almost any shape, carve even intricate sculptural forms and polish large surfaces in a relatively short period of time. Because of the uniqueness of glass as an amorphous material, certain limitations apply to the ability to machine it. Even well-annealed glass has some stress. Heat will aggravate the stress and cause the glass to crack. All glasses must be kept cool with water or cutting solution during any high-speed machine process.

The term "to cut" glass has many meanings.

1. To separate one piece of glass from another, such as a glazier would cut a piece of glass for a window or a stained-glass artist would cut many small pieces to fit together into a larger unit. Carbide or diamond-tipped cutting wheels are used to score the surface of the glass initiating a fracture line. Pressure is applied to the fracture line, causing the piece to separate. This technique can be used with practice to cut sheet glass up to 1" thick. (See cutting directions in "Slumping" section.)

2. To cut with a saw. There are many types and sizes of saws available on the market today with built-in cooling systems. The blades are most often diamond coated, but there are less expensive carbide blades on the market. The cutting action takes place by abrasion, as is true of all mechanical cutting of glass. Most saws used today by artists are either lapidary or masonry saws. The main difference in the cutting action is the type of blade used. For glass, a finer-grit continuous-rim blade gives a cleaner cut.

Marvin Lipofsky cuts into his blown forms, removing parts to open up and reveal the negative space. The sculptural pieces are shaped and ground, then sandblasted or acid polished. The cut-away parts are sometimes combined with the original form to create a new work of art.

Marvin Lipofsky cutting on diamond saw. (photo courtesy the artist, photo by Monica Lee)

145

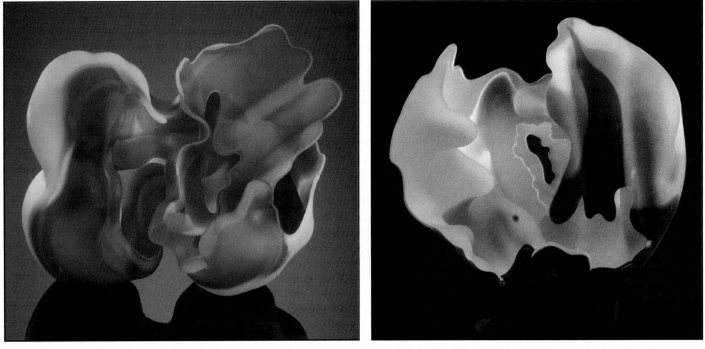

Marvin Lipofsky, "Pilchuck Group 1995-97 #4," blown at Pilchuck with help from Tom Kreager and team, finished in artist's California studio. (photo courtesy the artist, photo by M. Lee Fatherree)

Marvin Lipofsky, "Pilchuck Summer Series 1988-97 #23," 13-1/2" x 15-1/2" x 11-1/2", formed with help from Eric Bladholm, Tom Kreager and Dante Marioni, finished in artist's studio. (photo courtesy the artist, photo by M. Lee Fatherree)

Types of Saws

Cut off or **trim saws** have blades set in a recessed box for coolant. Blades range from 6" up to 10".

Slab saws have a built-in auto-power-feed system and can take blades up to 24" in diameter.

Chop saws have a sliding tray that can feed the work into an overhead blade in a variety of sizes.

Bandsaws are also available from a large industrial size and cost to smaller hobby versions.

Tile cutting saws are inexpensive diamond saws designed for cutting ceramic tile. They will work fine, especially if used with a finer saw blade.

Makita. The most remarkable means of cutting glass so far designed is a little 4" diamond-blade battery-operated saw

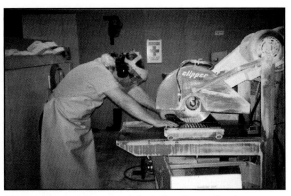

Doug Ohm at the saw. (photo by the author)

made by Makita, with a little plastic-bottle water-feed system. This saw can be used at on-site installations; horizontal or vertical, I suppose even upside down. The most impressive feature is its low cost. So many machines designed for glass work are very expensive and cumbersome in size, making it difficult for small studios to accommodate a variety of these tools.

The term "to cut" glass also means to cut and polish a design into the surface of a glass object. Very few contemporary artists are using this technique; however, it is still favored in Ireland, England and Scotland for decorative tableware. Waterford Crystal is the most popular example of cut glass. Cameo cutting is an ancient technique that involves both cutting and carving. Its history includes both lapidary and glass applications.

The process of grinding and polishing involves using a series of abrasive grains sliding across the surface of the glass object, removing tiny bits of material which appear as scratches. These scratches gradually decrease in size as finer grades of abrasive are used. Grinding of glass can be accomplished in many ways. There is a variety of machines designed to do most grinding jobs. You can, of course, do it the old-fashioned way–by hand.

Horizontal lapidary discs are available in cast iron or natural stone and are used with a slurry of silicon carbide or aluminum oxide. These machines are large, cumbersome and mostly out-of-date. They can often be purchased as used glass or lapidary equipment. The more modern version of the flat lap utilizes diamonds. Diamond-impregnated discs, which come in many types and grit sizes, are designed to fit machines from 12" to 24" in diameter.

Reciprolap or automatic vibrating laps are designed to abrade and polish flat surfaces automatically. A piece is loaded into the machine with the appropriate size grit, the machine is then turned on and away you go. The lap vibrates underneath the piece, simulating the action of lapidary discs.

80-grit grinding wheel, "Wheaton Village." (photo by the author)

Diamond lap wheel, at the Studio of the Corning Museum of Glass. (photo by the author)

Vertical wheels can be made from cork, horse hair or Spanish felt for polishing and silicon carbide or diamond wheels for grinding or bevel cutting.

Diamond lathes are vertical wheels mounted on a shaft. They can be used to cut and grind glass, especially punty marks and bevel edges of sheet or plate glass.

Wet-abrasive belt-machines, sometimes called glass-edging machines, are the most versatile machine for the small studio, as they require a simple belt change to increase or decrease the grinding sequence. Some polishing is possible with a cork belt. Sommer and Maca make a large floor model plus a smaller tabletop machine. Abrasive belts are available in grit sizes from 60-grit for rough grinding to 400-grit for semi-polish with a cork belt for finer polish. Diamond impregnated belts are also available for this machine at a much greater cost.

Marvin Lipofsky grinding on diamond-lathe. (photo courtesy of the artist, photo by Monica Lee)

Vertical wheel, the Studio of the Corning Museum of Glass. (photo by the author)

Hand held grinders also come in a variety of sizes. One version made in Germany is called "Flex." It's a water-fed, hand-held grinder with interchangeable diamond grit pads; it can be pneumatically or electrically powered. The stone-carving industry is a good source for this type of tool.

Flexible-shaft power tools are hand-held tools for the grinding and polishing of all types of materials. When used with diamond burrs, they are good for hand-grinding glass. The motor can be hung up, safely away from any coolant damage or electrical shock.

Dremels and other small hand-held grinding tools will also work. Since all machine grinding must be done with some type of coolant, the liquid can damage the motor and cause severe electrical shock if carelessly used.

The Old Fashioned Way. A slurry of abrasive grit applied to any glass surface by hand will eventually abrade the surface. It just takes a much longer time. Abrasive papers such as 3-M tri-mite (wet or dry) will also work in time.

Wet belt-grinder, the Studio of the Corning Museum of Glass. (photo by the author)

Fordam flex shaft. (photo by the author)

The grinding sequence goes from coarse grits through a series of finer or smoothing grits to a polishing sequence. The coarser the grit, the faster it cuts, but the surface is more deeply scarred for subsequent finer grinding. The procedure for grinding and polishing any surface is to replace the abrasive scratches with a succession of finer scratches until they are finally invisible. In each step it is important to remove all traces of the previous coarser scratches before going on to the next grit. Therein lies the tediousness of the task.

The single most important factor when grinding and polishing is lubrication. The heat generated when using any power tool is sufficient to crack glass. Water is most often used, although kerosene, cutting oil and commercial diamond coolants work well. Silicon carbide and aluminum oxide are the most common abrasive grits. Diamond-grits are much more costly. They all come in mesh size 60 through 600. The higher the number, the finer the grit.

Grinding Sequence

1. Begin with 60 or 80 grit to establish the basic shape of the area to be ground. If it is to be a flat plane, a small level held on top helps to establish proper alignment. Be sure to wash away all coarse grit before going on to the next size.
2. Change to the next size, 120 or 220 grit. Alter the direction of the cutting action if possible. Some material will still be removed; continue until all visible scratches from the coarser grit are gone. Wash away all grit.
3. Change to the next grit size 320/400, again altering the direction until all of the previous scratches are gone. A semi-polish will be visible. Wash.
4. The final abrasive grit is 600. The more time spent on the 600 grit, the faster subsequent polishing steps will be accomplished. The surface should have a dull sheen and no visible scratches.

Polishing

Polishing glass requires a series of finer abrasives and cork, horsehair or felt wheels turning at a very slow speed (380 rpm). Each grade of polishing compound should have its own wheel, as it is impossible to remove the coarser compounds when changing to a finer powder. Optical polishing compounds like pumice and cerium oxide are the most common polishing compounds; they're available in coarse, medium, fine and extra-fine powders. It would be wonderful if every artist who wanted to polish glass had a large 16" floor-model polishing wheel. For those who do not, there are smaller felt wheels to fit bench grinders and discs to fit variable speed drills, even smaller ones to fit dremels and flex shafts.

Polishing sequence
1. Wet the wheel thoroughly. Mix water with fine powder pumice to form a thick paste.
2a. With wheel: Hold object up to the wheel with a light pressure with one hand while feeding the pumice paste onto the wheel with the other. Take care not to allow the object or the wheel to become to dry. Heat generated from the pressure could cause the glass to crack.
2b. With hand-held felt discs: secure object so that it won't move from vibration and pressure. Apply paste to object, small amounts at a time. Using a hand-held tool on slow speed, apply disc with a light amount of pressure in a rotating motion to the object.
   Continue adding paste each time it appears to look dry.
3. Wash often to check progress. The object should have a fine sheen with no visible scratches.
4. Repeat steps 1-3, this time with extra-fine cerium oxide. The object should have a bright shiny finish by this time. Congratulations!!!

Drilling Holes

Drill press with water-feed attachment. (photo by the author)

Machines to drill holes in glass can range from tiny laser units to large abrasive tubes mounted on special drill presses. Holes can be sandblasted through glass or even water jet drilled. The oldest version of a glass drill bit is a spear point glass drill bit. These are still available today in tungsten carbide and must be used at a very slow speed (600 RPM) or with an old-fashioned hand drill.

The most common method is a core drill bit used on a drill press. One type of core bit is a brass or steel tube used with an abrasive slurry like silicon carbide. A retainer ring is built around the area where the hole is intended and filled with a lubricant. The abrasive grit is added, then the drill bit is lowered in place. The abrasive does the cutting. Diamond-coated bits are more costly, but much more efficient and tidy. They should always be used with a drill press, as they break easily.

There are several versions. Very small bits, 1 mm to 3 mm, are coated solid-steel shanks and are externally lubricated. Diamond-coated core bits can be externally or internally lubricated with a drill-head coolant-feeder.

Abrasive blasting or sandblasting. Sand breaks down very quickly to a very fine powder that is hazardous to your lungs. The minute particles of silica enter little cavity's on the walls of your lungs, (literally billions of them) and they stay there forever. Any abrasive use of sand must be done with a respirator. Silicon carbide (carborundum) or aluminum oxide can be used to abrade glass and also carve deep cuts and grooves, but does not pose as great of a risk of silicosis. It is wise to practice good safety habits and to get in the habit of wearing a respirator at all times.

The principle of abrasive blasting is that an abrasive material is propelled through a nozzle by compressed air. The PSI (pounds per square inch) of air passing through the hose is controlled by pressure gauges. The PSI required for a specific job depends on the size and type of equipment, plus the type of cutting or frosting required. The nozzle size will also be a factor in the desired finish. Small deep cuts will require a small nozzle with about 80 to 100 PSI. A general overall frost on most types of glass could be obtained with a larger nozzle and about 60 PSI.

Abrasive blast equipment can be as large as a room or as tiny as an airbrush. Room-size systems require the use of a special hood with an independent oxygen supply, much like a scuba diver would wear. Even the tiny air brush types require full face protection. Most cabinet blasters recycle the grit and have some type of dust collection system. Even then, a respirator should be worn as fine particles of dust escape from the cabinet and dust collector. The gun where the air and grit are mixed can be a trigger type or it can be controlled by a foot pedal. Portable units are available, some are inexpensive. They consist of a bucket to contain the abrasive, a trigger gun that has one hose connected to the air supply and another connected to the pipe at the bottom of the bucket. Gravity

Small sandblaster with compressor and dust collection system. (photo by the author)

Large sandblaster with pressure pot and dust collection system. Creative Glass Center of America/Wheaton Village. (photo by the author)

drops the grit to the bottom and small air holes in the pipe draw the grit into the gun. This type does not recycle the grit. Sand is the least expensive, but proper protection is a must. Another type of portable unit is a pressure blaster. This type unit forces air and grit through the nozzle together under tremendous pressure. It works much faster, especially when cutting through thick glass.

Air compressors provide the air under pressure for the abrasive blast system. At least a 5-horsepower compressor that delivers 15-20 CFM is required to run a small unit at 90 PSI. Sears, building supply companies and even some hardware stores sell compressors. Heavy-duty industrial workhorses can often be found as used equipment for very little money. If your needs are not extensive or you wish to try before you buy, you might check your local yellow pages for sand-blasting-rental. Your local glass supply company might have equipment and be willing to rent it or do it for you. An exhaust system is also very important as the particle dust is in the environment even from state-of-the-art units with dust collecting systems.

Assembly Techniques

Glues for glass: Now that the piece is almost finished, it probably needs to be assembled in some way, attached to a base, made so that it can stand or even be hung up. The variety of assemblage techniques is vast; however, there are some things that just won't work. A more traditional means of construction would include glazing and cementing. Glazing means to fit with glass, as for instance, a pane or panel of glass installed into a frame or casement. Glazing techniques can vary greatly. Innovative architectural techniques are expanding the range of prefabricated materials designed to be fit with glass. Industrial machining of glass has also increased the materials' ability to be assembled into precarious configurations. Cements, both traditional and new plastic-based concrete mixes, allow for a great freedom of design. Glass can now be bolted to glass, or any other material and all sorts of metal findings can be used creatively.

Until recently, glue was a less than satisfactory method for attaching glass to glass or to any other surface with permanent expectations. This century saw advances in chemical technology that brought about adhesives like silicones, epoxies and the newer acrylics and UVs. The development of silicone adhesives has had the greatest impact on the emergence of large scale constructions like Larry Bell's "Iceberg and its Shadow." In Bell's work, the large sheets of glass are held together with silicone adhesive. The bond remains firm yet flexible, allowing a slight

Larry Bell, "The Cat Part II," 1981, 1/2" clear glass coated with Iconel, 12 panels (photo courtesy of the artist, photo by Mary Bachmann)

degree of movement, which is good because glass is flexible. It can crack if held tightly in rigid compression. Another practical aspect of silicone adhesives is that bonds are easily separated when cut with a razor blade, allowing large temporary installations to be easily disassembled. It is still the best glue to use if work is to be permanently cited outdoors, especially in the cold North and North East of the country. In cases of severe contrasts in weather, the glass will expand and contract. Also water can freeze around joints causing both glue and glass to crack if it can't move.

Now there are two other good glues for glass, but each one has limitations. Most epoxies do not work well; if they do stick, they turn yellow in time. Epoxy systems are thermoplastic (heat set). Two parts, usually equal, are mixed together generating heat that activates the bonding action. One part contains metal particles that cause the discoloration when exposed to light.

A Texan developed an ultra-pure epoxy in his garage for conservation use that did not yellow. Hyxtal-NYL-1 is a very special epoxy and must be handled accordingly. First, it was selected by the British Museums' conservator to rebuild the Portland Vase, so it has distinguished honors. Second, it has a list of don'ts a mile long. Third, it's expensive; for a brief time, some thought it was going to be permanently out of stock. It's around and works great for some things.

Hyxtal is mixed as a three-parts of A to one-part of B ratio. A gram scale is a must, as the measurement is by weight, and the ratio's accuracy is critical. Weigh accurately and mix thoroughly. Everything that comes in contact with the glue must be glass. Scientific glassware, shallow Petrie dishes, or small glass jars make good containers. Glass stirrers or finely-pulled glass rods, even thin strips of window glass will work; to make them, you will get some practice cutting glass. All surfaces to be glued must be squeaky clean, preferably with 99% pure isopropyl alcohol. Hyxtal takes about seven days (five in warm weather) to achieve bond strength. If you are propping up something to be glued, it better be stable. Sometimes you can move it after a few days. If the bonded area is small or the joint is precarious, never ship it until after the full seven days. There are some shortcuts taken to speed-up the process that involve heating the mixture in a water bath to 120F for a few minutes or warming the article to about 90F after 36 hours. I don't recommend either step if a precarious joint is in question. Have patience, let it alone for seven days.

If the piece is neither yellow nor dark in color, try an ultraviolet glue instead. UVs, as they are known, contain a chemical called a photoinitiator. When a photoinitiator is exposed to the proper wavelength UV light, a reaction occurs causing the adhesive to set-up and cure. Depending on the type of UV adhesive, the light source and the size of the piece, a cure can take just a few minutes. Most do take longer, because the high-intensity lights are very expensive and out of the range of most studio artists.

Intensity or brightness and spectral output or electromagnetic wave energy are two factors determining how fast a UV lamp will cure a product. Intensity is controlled by the power of the lamp, the distance from the joint to be glued, the type of reflector and the age of the bulb (bulbs lose intensity with age). Spectral output is necessary in the 200-400 nanometer (nm) range.

Long wavelengths. Most lamps are measured at 365 nm. There are several types of light sources available: fluorescent blacklight lamp or blacklight blue bulbs. Spectroline makes several versions in the 365 nm spectrum. Mercury vapor lamps are made with a quartz glass sleeve, argon and a small amount of liquid mercury. A high voltage causes an arc which heats up and creates mercury gas. The mercury gas emits sufficient wavelengths in the recommended UV range. The mercury lamps have a higher wattage, thus a faster cure.

The sun. The sun works best at high noon on the longest day of the year somewhere near the Equator. Locktite does make a product called Crystal Clear for general consumers that can be cured with a low intensity UV light. There is also a remote possibility that your dentist might lend you one for a day or two.

A very valuable function of both Hyxtal and UV glue is conservation and repair. A thin mixture of either can be fed into cracks, air bubbles and small checks. It helps to pre-warm the area first with a hair dryer or light bulbs. Place a small amount directly over the crack and allow it to be absorbed. Capillary action should draw the liquid into the crack. Many masterpieces have been saved in this manner.

Orasol dyes from Ciba-geigy work well in coloring the Hyxtal and UV glues and come in wonderful bright, light-stable colors. They are available as a powder from either source of supply. To use, they are mixed at a ratio of less than 5% volume. Mix thoroughly until all of the powder is dissolved. I recommend testing for intensity of color before using.

There are a few other glues that seem to work for odd jobs. A hot glue gun can temporarily tack glass to glass or other surfaces. E6000 seems to work for pinbacks and other small metal parts. Tacky glue, of all things, works on glass to wood or other porous surfaces and Elmer's glue burns out clean, when fired, for kiln work. Super Glue just does not make it to the Glass Glue Hall of Fame.

Jon Kuhn is a master of creating shimmering, glittering, reflective optical illusions. He makes intricate inner structures by bonding small pieces of optical quality diacroic glass together. These small iridescent paintings are cased by bonding together blocks of crystal-clear optical glass. The sculpture is then laboriously ground and polished. Highly-polished surfaces reflect an infinite array of colors...like seeing the aurora borealis.

Sidney Hutter also spends a lot of time grinding and polishing. He uses plate glass for his metaphoric vase forms which are assembled by stacking plates of water-clear glass, often with color in between the layers. His vessels allude to a container; however, they are either silhouettes of a vase or negative vase form created by the stacked glass. Each layer is carefully planned, cut and polished to precise dimensions before assembly. Color dyes play an important role in creating a sense of mystery as the highly-polished surfaces break-up and reflect light.

Reference

1.   Wills, Geoffrey, *English Looking Glasses*, "A Journey to Paris in the Year 1698," Dr. Martin Lister, p. 61, A.S. Barnes and Co., 1965.

155

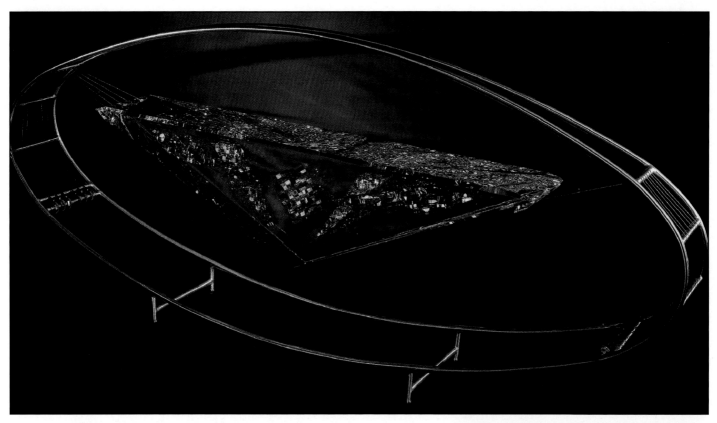

Jon Kuhn, "Olympic Vision 1998," 38" wide x 9-3/4" high x 3-1/4" deep, frame 58" wide x 24" high x 8-1/2" deep, glass. (photo courtesy of the artist, photo by Jackson Smith)

Sidney R. Hutter, "Vase #28/04," 1995, cut, polished, dyed and laminated plate glass 16.5" high x 8.5" wide x 8.5" deep. (photo courtesy of the artist)

Sidney R. Hutter, "Cubic Heart Vase #7," 1996, cut, polished, dyed and laminated plate glass 15" high x 12.5" wide x 12.5" deep. (photo courtesy of the artist)

Section 8

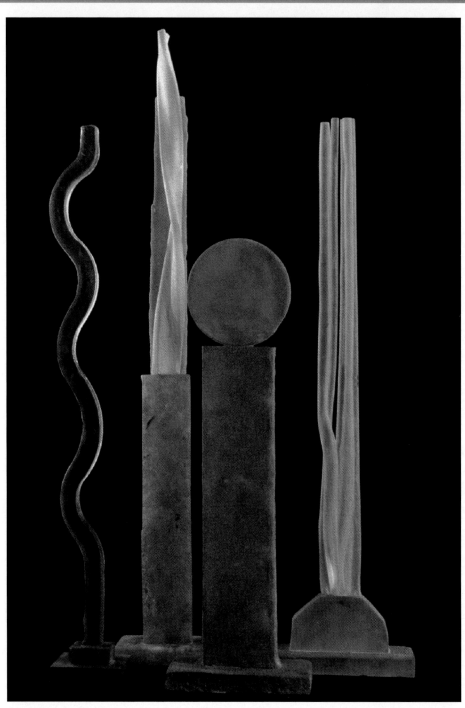

Lucartha Kohler, "Primary Totems," 48" high x 6" wide x 4" deep, glass tables. (photo courtesy of artist)

A Material in the Service of Art

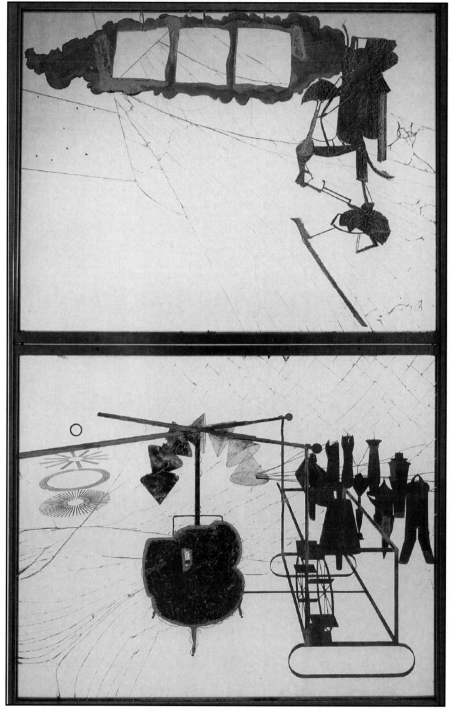

Marcel Duchamp, "Large Glass," 1952-98-1. (Philadelphia Museum of Art, bequest of Katherine S. Dreier)

The common thread uniting the work of all artists who choose to use glass as a material for the creation of works of art exists in the very nature of glass itself. The many dichotomies of the character of glass and the diverse physical properties of the material have introduced a new vocabulary. Adjectives such as transparent, translucent and reflective are translated into a personal language of individual artists, as are metaphors such as "illusion" and "illumination."

The illusionistic qualities of glass are pushed to their ultimate experience in Marcel Duchamp's enigmatic "The Large Glass" or "The Bride Stripped Bare by Her Bachelors, Even." This work is both a technical feat and an esthetic experience. Duchamp's ability to destroy old formats for the creation of new forms has given him a unique position in shaping current directions in contemporary art. The total body of Duchamp's work has yet to be completely understood, allowing art students and historians much room for creative speculation. For Duchamp, glass was a material perfectly suited for creative expression. His fascination with glass as a material has been documented in his many writings. According to Duchamp scholar, Ulf Linde, "The Green Box" contains reference to "The Large Glass" as a "Poeme en Verre." The visual elements of "The Large Glass" exist as symbols, as do the large transparent panels of glass including the accidental fractures which declared its completion.

Many artists and poets have found the metaphysical aspects of glass to be experiential and expressive. It exists, but it doesn't; it is strong, yet fragile; it can be a liquid frozen in space and time, or it can be dense and opaque like metal. It can be fire and it can be ice. It's directly influenced by and responds to, the quality of light; as light reacts and interacts with glass it can literally become a rainbow, or it can gather a beam of light and create a rainbow.

> *It's of the Earth*
> *Formed by Fire*
> *Shaped by Air*
> *Made pure by Water*

According to ancient alchemists, the transformation of images via materials represents the "Philosopher's Stone." Glass exists metaphysically as a profound manifestation of all the elements.

The Surrealist movement found both subject and object in the mystery of glass. In 1965, the Museum of Modern Art in New York City presented an exhibition entitled "Sculpture in Glass." This was an exhibition of 33 objects designed by Jean Arp, Max Ernst and Pablo Picasso and executed in the glass factories in Murano, Italy. This project was organized by Venetian glass dealer Egidio Costantini, to restore art to the craft of glassblowing. Object in art, art object, art, all aspects of glass can be explored as personal metaphor.

Joseph Cornell saw glass as a means to isolate and protect his very personal worlds, as well as to symbolize or represent aspects of his very soli-

Joseph Cornell, "Glass Rabbit Box," 1950, mixed media box construction, 11" high x 6-1/2" wide x 4-1/4" deep. (photo courtesy of the ACA Gallery)

160

 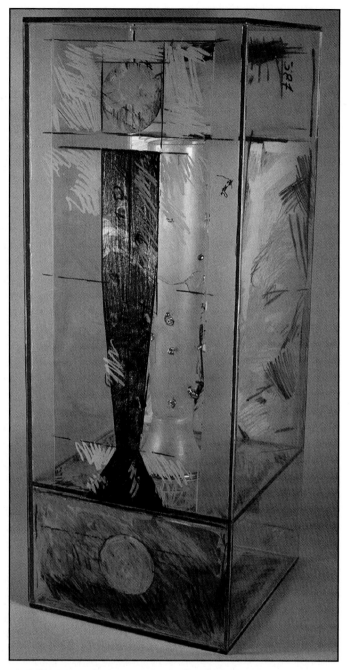

Henry Halem, "Profiled Vessel," 1997, glass, oil stick, ink, gold leaf, acrylic ink. (photo courtesy of the artist)

Another view of Henry Halem's "Profiled Vessel."

tary vision. Objects, bottles, wineglasses, sand (the basic element in forming glass) and reflective surfaces such as mirrors and tinted glass all re-occur in Cornell's work. All of Cornell's objects serve to take the viewer along with him on his imaginary journeys through time and space.

Henry Halem, is another artist who uses glass to isolate and contain a vision. He combines elements that refer to artifacts of ancient cultures, espe-

161

Italo Scanga, "Glass Tree," 25" x 10" x 10"; "Glass Flame," 14" x 6" x 6", 1997. (photo courtesy of the artist)

cially ancient glass. His work imitates museum display cases that separate and make special those objects that were intended for every day use. The glass vessel is a personal, yet universal symbol. As in Cornell's work, there is but an allusion to containment. The frame and glass serve to contain and separate the art from the viewer. Techniques derived from collage-assemblage traditions give symbolic meaning to each object, yet changing its original form to create a new and more universal meaning.

Metaphorically, glass as object is also incorporated into the work of Italo Scanga. Best known for his constructions combining high art and religious images, he uses techniques derived from collage-assemblage traditions and gives symbolic meaning to objects influenced by his Italian heritage. Many years ago, he was one of the first non-glass artists invited to be artist-in- residence at the Pilchuck School. He was responsible for developing the current program that invites painters and sculptors to experience glass as a material for their art.

Just as philosophy and social issues affect the directions of art, so does technology. 20th century cities are canyons of glass, steel and concrete. Sheet glass can be formed to span great distances and to withstand extreme environmental conditions. Mary Shaffer bends industrial plate glass, sometimes combining it with cast bronze in large scale sculpture installations.

Molten glass can be cast into complex and monumental forms. Architecture has transformed our world into one of transparent and reflective surfaces and made glass a very influential and integrated part of our lives. This advanced technology has freed glass from environmental restrictions and has allowed glass sculpture to go beyond the object. Glass can function like a jewel in the cold utilitarianism of today's urban architecture.

Mary Shaffer, "Mamoure I.S.," 1992, glass, bronze, copper and steel, 75" x 65" x 12". (private collection, photo by George Erml)

The work of a Swede, Edvin Ohrstrom, illustrates the monumental capabilities of glass sculpture. A 57-meter tall column is installed in Stockholm where winters are most severe. This pillar consists of three major forms, weighs 130 tons and contains 80,000 units of glass held together by stainless steel. The construction was designed to resist weather, wind and water, but, if need be, the units of glass are replaceable. An internal lighting system illuminates the glass during Sweden's long nights. This column, completed in 1974, and others of similar construction surely establish the reality of glass as a material for monumental and environmental sculpture.

Edvin Ohrstrom, "View of Studio," 1984. (photo by the author)

Edvin Ohrstrom, "Glass Column at Sergals Torg," Stockholm City, 1974, 57 meters high.
(photo by the author)

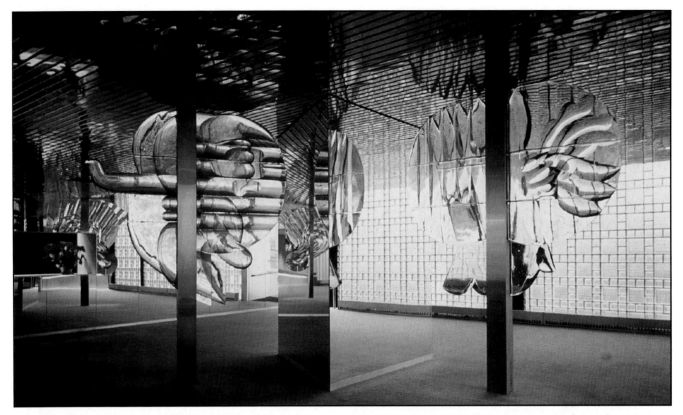

Stanislav Libinsky and Jaroslava Brychtova, "Meteor, Flower and Bird," 1978-1980, 80.3.18. (photo courtesy of the Corning Museum of Glass)

The technical procedures and equipment required to cast large volumes of glass for architectural scale works have been limiting for most artists. Traditionally in Eastern Europe there has been an open collaboration between the artist and industry. In 1920, a school of glassmaking was founded at Zelezney Brod, former Czechoslovakia, to cooperate with the Zelenobrodske Sklo Glassworks. Stanislav Libinsky along with his wife Jaroslava Brychtova have been pioneers in the field of glass object in architectonic space. Professor Libinsky assumed the post of director of the school of glassmaking. His wife Brychtova, daughter of the cofounder of the school, began her career as a sculptor assisting her father in experiments with molten glass. Since the early 1960s, they have worked together to realize large-scale glass sculptures. A significant factor influencing the direction of their work has been the relationship of glass to architecture, collaborating with architects to develop the atmosphere necessary for glass sculpture to function.

Gene Koss has been casting large-scale works of art in glass and metal for a long time. The roots of his work are traced to his agrarian heritage with massive steel elements looking like sophisticated farm machinery. In the 1970s, when "process art" was the rage, he developed elaborate glass-forming devices he calls gizmos. Molten glass is ladled or poured in some fashion into a machine where it was manipulated in one way or another. These devices rarely survive the process intact. When they do, they're wonderful.

Gene Koss, "Plow," 1992, cast glass, steel, neon, 13 feet high x 15 feet wide. (photo courtesy of the artist)

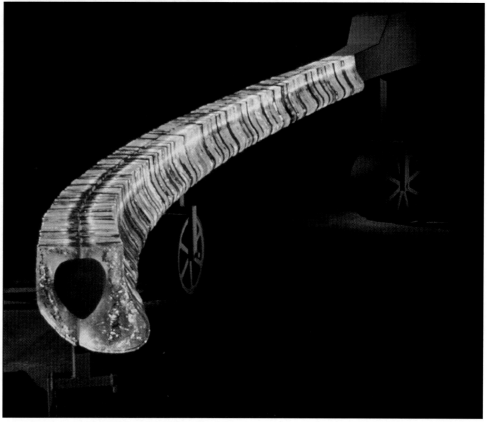

Gene Koss, "Night Harvester," 1995 cast glass, steel, neon, 9 feet x 28 feet x 3 feet. (photo courtesy of the artist)

Earth artists and environmental sculptors often found industrial glass and mirrors a challenging material to serve their purpose. Robert Smithson was a dynamic avatar whose influences continue to change the directions of contemporary art. Even before his untimely death in 1973, he had already established a precedent for altering the formal concepts embraced by contemporary art by redefining space.

Natural crystals were important to Smithson, crystalline matter for him held the key to understanding the concept of entropy (unavailable energy). This was one of the primary concerns he expressed during his very short career. In "Glass Stratum," the frozen-liquid nature of glass in contrast to the ordered molecular structure of crystals is at once a conflict. Visually, the ordered layering of glass represents the orderly arrangement of molecules in crystalline forms, in contrast to the illusionistic fluid sense of movement created by refracted light: conflict and contradiction. Again, a contrast between appearance and reality, illusory and illustrative of the nature of visual perception.

Robert Smithson, "Glass Stratum," 1967, 17-3/4" high x 12" wide x 84" long. (photo courtesy of the Robert Smithson Estate, John Weber Gallery)

Light is an important element of any sculptural statement. Light and shadow play an important role in defining real space and illusionistic space. Light can shape space without defining it and can alter form as the quality of light changes, the traditional sense of sculpture, occupying only mass and volume, is destroyed. The concept of light as a vehicle for experience was expressed by Chris Wilmarth: "Light gains character as it touches the world; from what is lighted and who there is to see. I associate the significant moments of my life with the character of light at the time. The universal implications of my original experience have located in and become signified by kinds of light. My sculptures are places to

Christopher Wilmarth, "Gnomms Parade #2," 1978, glass, steel, 90" high x 28" wide, private collection. (photo courtesy of The Studio for the First Amendment, photo Eric Pollitzer)

Christopher Wilmarth, "New Ninth," 1978, glass, steel, 32" high x 48" wide, private collection. (photo courtesy of The Studio for the First Amendment, photo Eric Pollitzer)

generate this experience compressed into light and shadow and return them to the world as a physical poem."[1]

Light, color, volume and space are all concerns of artists who choose glass as a material to realize their creative visions. Color and light creates real and illusionistic volume; existing in space as reality, yet existing as shadows–another form of reality. The quality of light determines the density of volume. The abstract force of light as energy used as a tool by the sculptor to create

Carol Cohen, "Little Compton," painted glass, wood box, 60" high x 72" wide x 20-1/2" deep. (photo courtesy of the artist)

reality is a unique phenomenon. To Carol Cohen, layering of images to create an illusionistic experience of volume is further refined by controlling the translucency, transparency and image placement on the glass. She builds images with paint, one layer at a time. The combined layers then become the whole picture.

The transparency of glass allows the environment to become one with the form. Larry Bell has used this quality to build imaginary landscapes. "The Cat, Part II" creates a world, both to view and to become a part of. The illusion of density occurring through the heavy surface coating, in contrast to the illusion of space where the coating is more transparent, creates an environment as diverse as our own "real" world.

The artist as architect of imaginary civilizations, creator of metaphoric spaces and builder of enigmatic structures is both

Larry Bell, "The Cat Part II," 1981, glass, coated with Iconel 12, panels, four 6" x 8" and eight 6" x 6".
(photo courtesy of the artist, photo Mary Bachman)

Mario Merz, "Double Igloo: Alligator with Fibonacci Numbers to 377," 1979, mixed media, private collection. (photo courtesy of the Sperone Westwater Gallery)

primitive and modern. He is a prophet of events forthcoming and is a reminder of events forgotten. Mario Merz is such an artist; he is an architect of the enigmatic. His "Double Igloo; Alligator with Fibonacci Numbers to 377" is both a structure with symbolic interpretation and a structure with literal significance. Its existence is both real and referential. Merz, builder of igloos, expresses the nomadic nature of the artist within the context of artistic construction. His igloos, built according to the process of growth, refer to the dynamic nature of organic development. The nomad, moving from one context to another for survival, embraces social, economic and spiritual ideology expressed through the process of building.

The igloo represents a cultural entity relating to the whole of society. Materials used for the building process are casual yet referential. The glass skin of the igloo expresses a duality of character. The ephemeral nature of the structure and the implied significance of nomadic life is evident in all his constructions. Merz's expression of this infinite growth process is directly related to the work of Leonardo da Pisa, later known as

Fibonacci, a medieval mathematician and nomadic wanderer who lived around 1200 AD. According to the Fibonacci System (he discovered it while breeding rabbits), a numerical progression exists that represents infinite growth. Each number is the sum of the preceding two: 1, 1, 2, 3; 5, 8, 13; 21, 34, 55 and so on. Neon acts as a sign, a number or as a spear of radiant light that penetrates the space, drawing attention to the definition of light as energy; sometimes redefining an object, sometimes canceling its existence. A paradox; a cancellation of systems within a system.

An enigma was also involved in Pike Powers' "Four Acts in Glass," shown at the American Craft Museum in 1997, based on her experiences at Coney Island. This installation presented a series of sideshow vignettes like little stages containing paintings with a folk art or outsider art quality. Each stage contained shelves with colorful figures displayed in solid glass specimen jars. The preserved side show freaks presented an eerie sense of the macabre. In contrast, the naive beauty of the paintings were paradoxically juxtaposed with the weird, grotesque specimens.

Reference

1. Exhibition catalog: "Christopher Wilmarth, Nine Clearings for a Standing Man," Wadsworth Atheneum, Hartford, CT, November 1974-January 1975.

Pike Powers, "Sideshow Installation: Twinisms," 1997, 10 feet high x 12 feet wide, glass, paintings and wood. (photo courtesy of the artist, photos by Eva Heyd)

Pike Powers, "Sideshow Installation: Wits End." (photo courtesy of the artist, photos by Eva Heyd)

Pike Powers, "Sideshow Installation: Whaling Museum." (photo courtesy of the artist, photos by Eva Heyd)

Pike Powers, "Sideshow Installation: Strange Girls and Old Men." (photo courtesy of the artist, photos by Eva Heyd)

Pike Powers, "Sideshow Installation: Snacks." (photo courtesy of the artist, photos by Eva Heyd)

Lucartha Kohler, "Glass House," 8 feet high x 5 feet wide x 4 feet deep, glass and steel. (photo by the author)

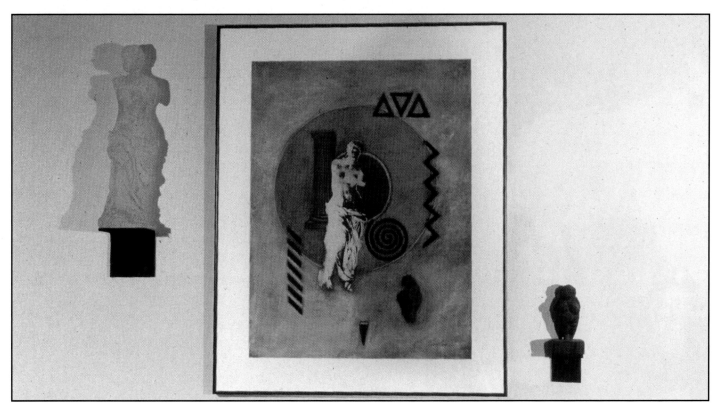

Lucartha Kohler, "Venus Venus," 40" high x 40" wide x 4" deep, glass, steel, drawing. (photo by the author)

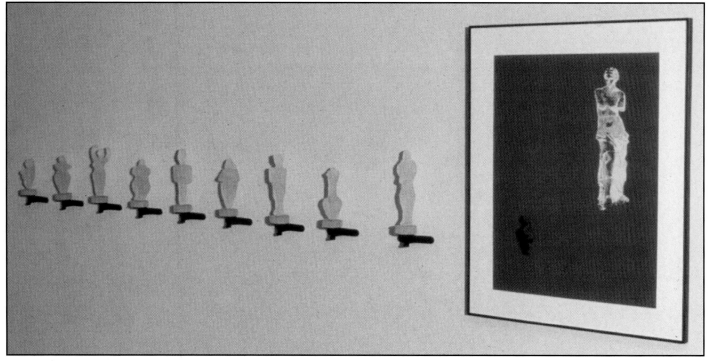

Lucartha Kohler, "They Call Her Venus," 40" high x 144" wide x 3" deep, glass, steel, drawing. (photo by the author)

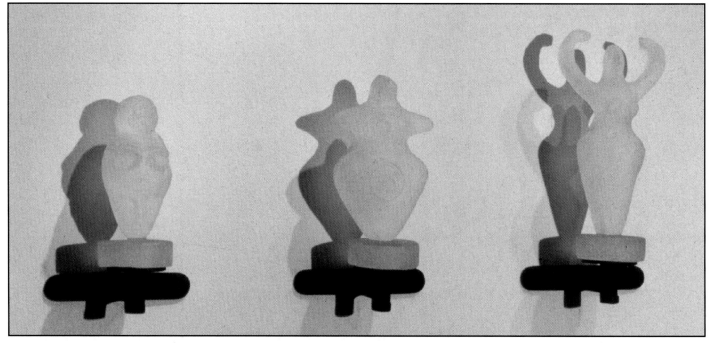

Close-up of Lucartha Kohler's, "They Call Her Venus." (photo by the author)

Lucartha Kohler, "Ancient Images of Womanhood," 24' wide x 24" x 10" wide (photo courtesy of the author)

Close-up of Lucartha Kohler's, "Ancient Images of Womanhood."

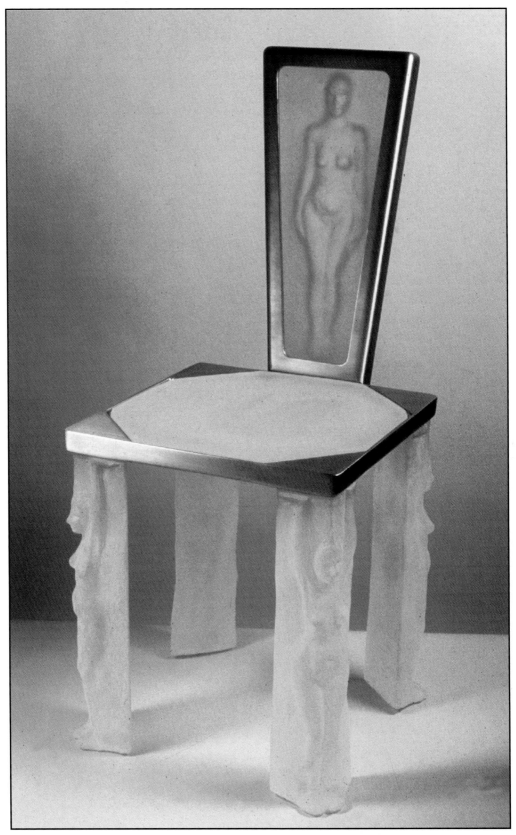

Lucartha Kohler, "Seat for a Goddess," 36" high x 15" wide x 17" deep, glass and stainless steel. (photo by the author)

Lucartha Kohler, "The Language of the Goddess," 16" high x 20" wide x 12" deep, glass. (photo by the author)

Lucartha Kohler, "Adam and Eve Goblets," 12" high x 3" diameter. (photo courtesy of the artist)

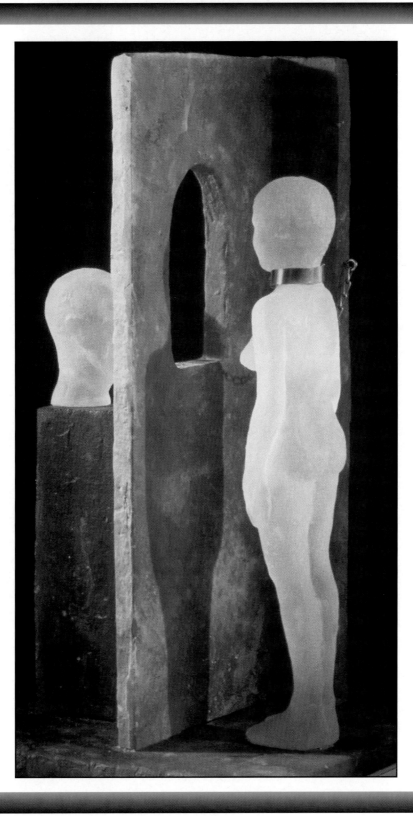

Molds

(see detailed step-by-step directions in "Pate de verre" section):

This is the least expensive and most often used mold formula by glass artists for casting:

50% plaster (pottery plaster or plaster of Paris)
50% silica flour (200 mesh flint)

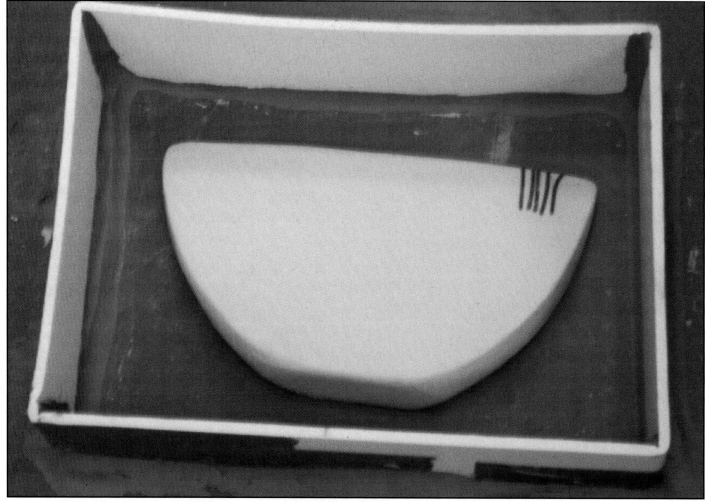

Wall built around clay model. (Mold by Lea Topping; photos by the author)

1. An original or positive form needs to be modeled in clay or wax.
2. When the form is ready; a wall is built around the positive object. Allow at least 1" around each side of the form and 2" above it. Secure the walls to your base. Next, seal around all of the walls with wet clay.

186

Plaster cast into mold walls.

Clay removed from mold and mold cleaned.

3. When the wall is secure enough, you can begin to mix the mold material. To ensure consistent results, weigh the plaster and the water, with a ratio of 1 pound of water to 1-1/2 pounds of plaster/silica. Note: 1 pint of water weighs 1 pound.

4. You add the dry mix to the water by gently sifting the powder onto the surface of the water until you have a dry island in the center of the water. Let it stand and soak for 3-4 minutes. Then begin to mix, making sure all of the lumps are dissolved. When mixing large amounts at a time, a paint mixer attachment can be used on an electric drill. You want the mixture to have a creamy consistency.

5. Once the plaster/silica mix is set up, (it takes 20 minutes or so) and the mold is cool and rigid to the touch, you can remove the flask and begin to "dig" out the clay or steam out the wax.

6. When the mold is clean, it is ready to fill with glass and fire.

Two or More Part Molds

The best positive model material for making multi-part molds is water-base clay. Clay allows you to insert shims directly into the material to make dividing walls. For solid materials, clay walls can be built. The most difficult task in making a multi-part mold is determining where to place the parting line. When looking at a model that needs a two- or more part mold, imagine pulling a rigid mold straight away from a given area. If this can't be done, a dividing line must placed in such a way to allow for that area to pull away. Shims are very thin strips of metal or plastic, tin or copper roof flashing makes great shims. Save them, as they can be used over and over.

Directions are for a two-part mold made from water-base clay:

1. Divide the model in two parts. Make a line where the shims are to be placed with a sharp tool.
2. Insert shims into the clay along the marked line. This will divide the object in half (see Step 1 photo). Lay the model flat with clay supporting the shims from underneath (see Step 2 photo).
3. Mix sufficient mold material to cover half of the mold to a thickness of 1". Allow the mold material to thicken a bit as you will be slush-coating the model. It is possible to make a box for this step, but it's time consuming and not really necessary (see Step 3 photo).
4. Allow mold mixture to set up. When it is hard, remove the shims.

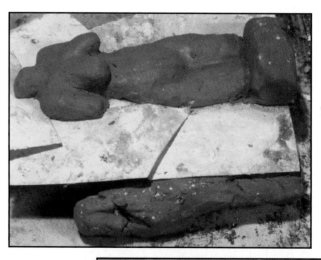

Two-part mold–Step 2

Two-part mold–Step 1
(photos by the author)

Two-part mold–Step 3

5. With a sharp tool. cut notches into the mold material. These will act as registers to lock the two halves properly together.
6. Coat all of the exposed mold material with Vaseline or oil soap. This step is very important. If you forget, the two halves will be forever stuck (see step 4 photo).
7. Mix sufficient mold material to coat the remaining half. Try to leave part of the dividing line visible. Allow to set-up.

Two-part mold–Step 4

Coat remaining half.

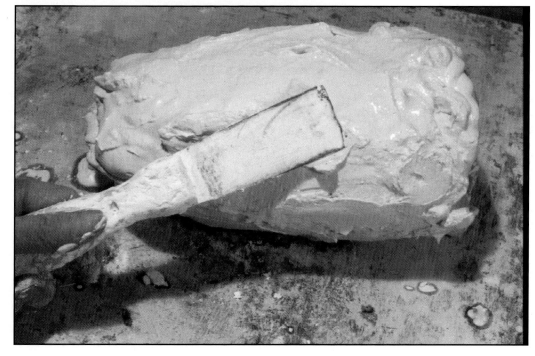

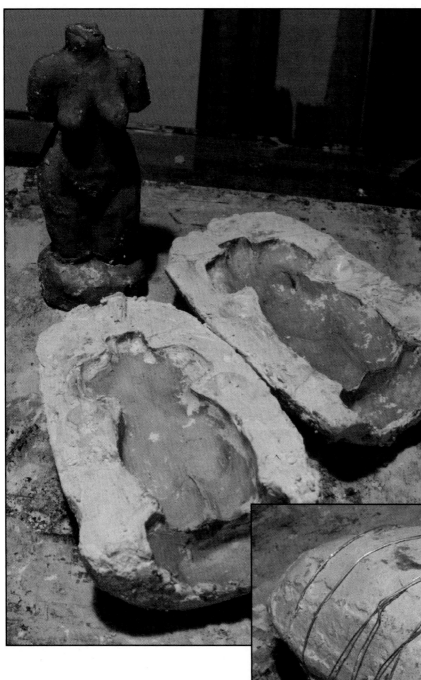

8. When the mold is hard, gently pry the two halves apart and remove the clay model (see Step 5 photo).
9. Put the two halves together and bind with stainless steel wire (see Step 6 photo).
10. Mix sufficient mold material to slush on a back-up coat over the wire. Make sure the parting seams are well covered. If the mold is large, use a back-up coat of the refractory mold mixture. Glass, when molten, can seep through cracks and be a mess.

Two-part mold–Step 5

Two-part mold–Step 6

Lost Wax Molds

1. Begin with a wax positive model. If the model has appendages and narrow areas that would present a problem for the glass to flow, air vents and sprues will need to be added. Air pockets can block glass from flowing into mold crevices (see Step 1 photo).

2. The wax model should be secured to a base. Wax has a tendency to float, because it is very light. A wall or flask is built around the model allowing about 1" mold thickness (see Step 2 photo).

3. Mix sufficient plaster/silica mold mixture to fill the flask. Allow to set up.

4. Remove the mold from the flask and steam out the wax (see Step 3). I use an old pressure cooker with a rubber hose attached to the steam vent on the lid. The mold is placed on a wire rack over a pan to catch the melting wax as it runs out of the mold. The rubber hose is inserted into the mold cavity. As the wax is eliminated, the hose can be pushed up farther into the cavity. Be careful doing this, as steam is quite hot and can cause burns.

Lost wax molds–Step 1: add air vents and sprues to wax. (photos by the author)

Lost wax molds–Step 2: flask built around model, fill mold with investment.

5. When all of the wax is removed it is ready to cast. If the mold is small it can go into the kiln as is. If it is large and requires a lot of glass, a back up coat of wire and stronger refractory material is recommended. (See also Frederick Carder's cire perdue)

Lost wax molds–Step 3: steam out the wax.

Refractory Molds

Kast-O-Lite 25 (by A.P. Green) or Hydracon 24 (by J.H. France) are lightweight refractory materials that are used for furnace building and other heat-treating applications. Other refractory manufacturers have similar products and most can be identified by comparing them to A.P. Green's product line. If handled carefully, this type of mold can hold up for many firings, provided there are no undercuts and the glass can drop freely out of the mold.

It is necessary with this material to begin with a model. This model can be of most any material, but moist clay works best. To prepare for the mold process, place the model on a base and make a retaining wall or flask. This flask could be of metal flashing, plastic, clay or wood. All joints should be sealed with moist clay to prevent leakage. A release agent, such as Vaseline, silicone or green soap, is brushed on all surfaces that come in contact with the castable refractory material. See also "plaster/silica, open-face mold" above.

The mixture is:
* 80%-90% Kast-O-Lite 25 or comparable product
* 10%-20% plaster, plaster of Paris, molding plaster or pottery plaster

The addition of 10%-20% plaster to the dry mixture will help the slurry set up faster and pick up any fine detail in the model. To mix the castable refractory, you begin with cool water in a bucket. About one-third of the volume needed to fill the mold flask. Sift the dry ingredients into the water until there is a dry island in the middle. Allow to settle for several minutes, then stir. You want the mixture to be rather thick, as too much water reduces the strength of the mold.

Vermiculite flakes in the refractory will float to the surface, so continue stirring until most of them settle. Pour the mixture into the mold flask and allow to set several hours or overnight. Remove the flask walls and the positive model carefully and allow to dry thoroughly, at least a week. The mold should be fired first to 1000F then allowed to cool to room temperature. The mold is then coated with high-fire kiln wash before using.

Dense Castable Refractory Mold

A more expensive mold, but one that lasts for many, many firings can be made from a denser refractory castable like A.P. Green, Mizzou or Greencast 94 or 97. The mold is made like the Kast-O-Lite formula above; however, I recommend using a U.S. Gypsum product called hydroperm instead of plaster, as it already contains some refractory material. There can't be any undercuts in the model or any way glass can get hung up in the mold. This mold must also be coated with high-fire kiln wash.

Back-up Molds

This dense castable formula also makes an ideal back-up for large plaster/silica molds. The plaster/silica mold is made according to directions above, then wrapped securely with stainless steel wire or hardware cloth. A 1" to 2" back-up coat of the dense refractory material is cast over the plaster/silica mold. It works best to cast the dense refractory material as soon as possible–while the plaster/silica mold is still wet. If that is not possible, the plaster/silica mold must be wetted down first as the dry mold will pull moisture out of the new mixture, altering the correct ratio of water to castable.

Anna Boothe's Mold for Pate De Verre

(courtesy of Anna Boothe)

A casting technique to form works made from finely crushed glass is combined with a binder to form a paste. The paste is packed into a refractory mold, allowing for specific localized color placement. The mold and glass are fired in a kiln. Here are the steps involved:

1. A positive form may be fabricated from clay, wax or a ready-made object.
2. Refractory mold formulas:
   a. 50% pottery plaster/50% silica by weight
   b. 1.5- to 2-parts plaster/silica mixture to 1-part water by volume If it needs reinforcement, add a handful of shredded fiberglass to mix
3. Build a flask wall around the positive model allowing at least 2" between the model and the wall. Mix enough mold material to fill flask about 2" deep. Allow to set up. Cut notches to register layers. Paint surface with a thin wash of clay slip (see Step 1).

Anna Boothe–Step 1: a positive form. (photos courtesy of Anna Boothe)

4. Continue building layers about 2" deep, coating with clay slip in between until the model is covered with mold material about 3" above the model (see Steps 2, 3 and 4).
5. Gently separate the rings and remove the positive model.
6. Colored glass frit can be localized in different areas of the mold at this time. Make a paste with frit, powder and Klyr-Fire binder a brand of methyl cellulose (see Step 5).
7. Put all of the layers back together with clay slip and seal with mold material (see Step 6).
8. If the mold is large, a wire reinforcement will be necessary, plus an outer shell of stronger refractory (see Step 7).

Anna Boothe–Step 2: build a flask wall, fill to about 2".

Anna Boothe–Step 3.

Anna Boothe–Step 4.

Anna Boothe–Step 5.

To fire, heat glass and mold at 100F per hour to 1000F. Vent oven 2" during this time. Soak at 1000F for one to three hours. Heat to 1550F until glass is melted. Charge mold with additional glass if necessary. When mold is filled, bring oven temperature to annealing point of the glass. Soak at this temperature for one hour for every 1/4" of glass thickness. (See chart for annealing rate)

Anna Boothe–Step 6.

Anna Boothe–Step 7.

Anna Boothe, "Confectionery Bowl," pate de verre, 1996, 5" high x 9-1/4" diameter. (photo courtesy of the artist; photo by Eric Mitchell)

One of Daniel Clayman's Formulas for Large Castings

(courtesy of Daniel Clayman)

Most of what Clayman does requires a face coat backed up by a bulk of material for firing strength. Percentages of mixing are by weight and not volume. All face coat material is put through a screen to rid it of large clumps. Face coats must be wetted as you prepare the outside coat. The mold must be completed on the same day, because the outside material will draw water from the face coat and not set properly.

Cristobolite is very strong and very expensive. It has a short working time, so you have to move fast after it's mixed. It leaves a very clean surface on the glass, so it makes a good face coat. It requires a backing coat.

Face coat–Cristobolite: water to Cristobolite is 1:2.5

Face coat–Ransom and Randolph 910: water to R&R 910 is 1:3

1. Pour the Cristobolite about 1" thick or apply it by hand about 1/2" thick.
2. After it set (about 1 hour), wet it with a spray bottle then mix the R&R 910 and hand pack it on the mold to a thickness of about 1-1/2".

The material should set at least 24 hours before firing. This material requires a very slow firing schedule and gives a stinky smell between 400F and 800F.

Plaster Molds: Frederick Carder's Formulas

(Courtesy of Paul Gardner: He was Frederick Carder's assistant at Steuben and worked with him when he was doing his casting experiments. He wrote the book The Glass of Frederick Carder and was an ardent supporter of the studio glass movement. I first met him in 1982, he was very supportive of my desire to cast glass; over the years, he shared some of Carder's information and experiences with me.)

Mold 1

1-part plaster (casting)
1-part fine silica (200 mesh)
1-part crushed mixture of above
    ingredients
Heat slowly to 100C, hold for several
    hours, then slowly to 300C

Mold 2

1-part Hydrocal
2-parts fine silica
3-parts Hydroperm
1-part fine silica
Dry slowly

Mold 3

1-part kaolin
1-part pottery plaster
0.02 part paper
0.02 part fibre-frax

Mix paper and fiber-frax with water in a blender. Strain pulp through a sieve into plaster/clay mixture.

Cire Perdue Frederick Carder[1]

1. The original statuette was modeled in clay. A modeling wax like plastelina was often used for the original model.
2. A plaster of Paris replica of the original clay statuette was made by the usual process employed by sculptors and ceramists.
*3. A "gelatin" mold was made from the plaster of Paris statuette. This mold, a reverse of the statuette, was in two or more sections, which fitted into an external plaster shell. The plaster shell was necessary to give the gelatin the support needed to keep it from collapsing.
4. A wax replica of the statuette was made from the gelatin mold. Usually only two or three wax castings could be taken from the gelatin mold. After that, the mold surface became worn and details of the modeling were lost.
5. The wax statuette was covered (or "invested") with the ceramic mold. This covering was a formula containing plaster and powdered calcined clay, the ingredients being mixed with water to form a liquid about the consistency of thick cream and poured over the wax model while still liquid. They were allowed to "set," which occurred in about 15 minutes as a result of the plaster content.
6. This mold was allowed to dry about 24 hours and then was placed over boiling water. The steam melted the wax, which ran out of the mold, leaving in the ceramic shell the molded impression (in reverse) of the original model. The ceramic mold was allowed to air-dry and then fired to a temperature high enough to drive off the volatiles in the plaster content.
7. Cold glass in the form of rods or lumps was now placed in the mold, and mold and glass were fired in a kiln to a temperature high enough to melt the glass and cause it to run into every portion of the mold.
8. Mold and glass were next cooled at a rate slow enough to anneal the solid mass of glass now filling the mold. Carder usually annealed his castings in the studio kiln he had constructed, which contained electric heating elements and allowed him to control the rate of cooling. Usually, this took from one to two days or longer, depending on the size of the glass casting. After cooling, the mold was broken away and the glass casting of the original model was revealed.

Carder's gelatin was composed of glue and glycerin melted together and poured while hot. When cool it made a pliable mold that could be peeled off the plaster model.

Zircar Mold Mix 6

Mold Mix 6 is a refractory mold material suitable for making some types of molds for casting and slumping glass. It works equally well casting with hot glass as it does for kiln casting. It is best to work from a wax positive as the material remains water soluble until fired. The best thing about the mold material is the ability to make lightweight molds that are resistant to thermal shock. The shell is built up in layers from 1/4" to 5/8" thick, depending on the size of the work to be cast. The material does not stick to the glass, giving the fired surface a better quality finish.

The material is costly. A lost wax mold situation in which the investment is broken away and destroyed might not be desirable. The fired material is quite rigid, possibly causing glass breakage upon removal of the positive from the investment. It is best suited for open-face drop-out molds, especially where size is a factor. It also works very well for slumping and blowing molds. I've been told it can also be used as sulfides or inclusions, encased in glass.

1. Molds can be made over most materials; however, wax is the best choice. Any other materials must be sealed with shellac. Unfired clay will leave a residue in the mold.
2. Coat with parting agent. Pam, Vaseline, green soap or Murphy's Oil Soap all make good parting agents.
3. Mold Mix 6 application. First coat is diluted with 35% water and brushed on. Allow to dry. After the first coat is dry, the Mold Mix 6 can be applied to the desired thickness. Small molds can be 1/4" thick; for larger molds 3/8" to 5/8" thick should be adequate.
4. Remove positive. Burn or melt the wax out. Do not steam, as the mold remains water-soluble until fired.
5. Fill with hot glass and anneal or fill with frit and fire to desired casting temperature, then anneal.

Ceramic Shell for Casting Glass[2]

The ceramic shell casting system was originally developed for casting metals. As a sculptor, familiar with the process for bronze casting, I began to experiment with various ceramic shell formulas for casting glass. The process does work; however, there are some limitations. The positive must be made from wax. Because the shell when fired is very strong, it is difficult to remove the casting–particularly if there are thick and thin areas (the thin areas of glass can break if the shell is tapped too hard). The shells must be built one layer at a time, allowing for a drying time in-between; thus the process is time consuming. The advantages of ceramic shell are the ability to withstand thermal shock which allows for ladling hot glass directly into a cold mold and the molds are strong and lightweight compared to other types of refractory investment.

The basic ingredient in the construction of a ceramic shell mold is colloidal silica, which, in combination with powdered silicates, form the ceramic shell. When one or more of these powders are combined with the colloidal silica a slurry mixture is created. This mixture is used in conjunction with a system of stucco coating of refractory powders and grains. This system of coating is repeated until a thickness of 1/4" to 1/2" is obtained. The shell is then flash-fired to remove the wax and to develop the strength of the ceramic shell.

1. The first step in the process of developing a ceramic shell mold is the wax original. The wax form may be made in several ways; it can be worked directly by modeling or assembled from pre-cast sheets and welded together with a hot tool, or it can be cast from a rubber or wet plaster mold.
2. After the wax form is ready, a pour cup or reservoir needs to be attached at the point where the mold is filled. It should be large enough to accommodate excess glass needed for kiln casting or wide enough to allow hot glass to flow.
3. The wax next needs to have some vents attached. The mold material is porous and allows for some gases and air to escape, but more air vents are required to prevent the flow of glass from being stopped by air pockets. Glass is much more viscous than metal and does not flow in the same manner. Sprues are needed to have glass flow from one area to another, but they must be thicker than those used for metal casting and designed to allow the glass to fill the mold by gravity flow. (See illustration on next page.)
4. A handle needs to be attached to the wax to facilitate handling of the shell during the coating process. A large nut and bolt installed in the cup works well.
5. Wax must be free from grease and parting agents. The pattern should be washed in alcohol, then allowed to dry.

Sectional View

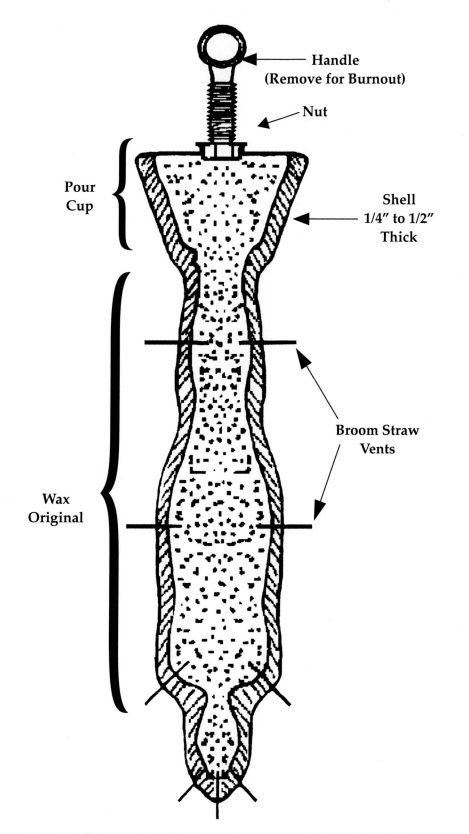

**Handle
(Remove for Burnout)**

Nut

**Pour
Cup**

**Shell
1/4" to 1/2"
Thick**

**Broom Straw
Vents**

**Wax
Original**

Drawing illustrating handle placement, pour cup and air vent system (broom straws).

Coating model with slurry mixture. (photo by the author)

The directions are for Shellspen Ceramic Slurry mixture, which comes in a premixed kit from the Johnson Atelier Sculpture Supply Catalog. It is the easiest to use as the slurry remains in suspension, unlike other refractory slurries. Ransom & Randolph makes a colloidal silica binder called Primcote. This slurry can be used with appropriate stucco grains including zircon.

If you find your glass is sticking to the shellspen shell, add about 10% zircon flour and thin the mixture with shellwet liquid for the first coat. Add about 10% zircon flour to the shellstuck stucco for the second coat.

Application procedure: Shellspen may be applied by dipping or by brushing. A minimum of six coats will be needed, allowing each coat to dry thoroughly in-between.

First coat: Shellspen alone (no stucco). Care should be taken to coat evenly and thoroughly as the first coat registers every detail. Hang by hook and allow to dry. Drying can be controlled by using an electric fan. Never apply heat, as the wax will expand and crack the shell.

Second coat: Pre-wet by brushing or misting with shellwet or distilled water. Apply Shellspen followed by fine shellstuck stucco. To apply the stucco use a fine sieve and a sprinkle motion. Allow to dry.

Third coat: Pre-wet, apply Shellspen followed by fine shellstuck stucco, dry.

Fourth and fifth coats: Pre-wet, apply Shellspen followed by medium shellstuck stucco, dry.

Sixth through ninth coats: Pre-wet, Shellspen followed by coarse shellstuck stucco. Allow to dry. Shell should be 1/4" thick for 5 pounds of glass. For heavier or larger shells, a thickness of 1/2" or more may be required.

Final coat: Shellspen alone, NO stucco.

Wax burnout: The wax may be eliminated from the shells by flash firing. The shell is placed directly in a furnace of 1800F to remove the wax before it expands. This will take a few minutes.

Burn Out Furnace

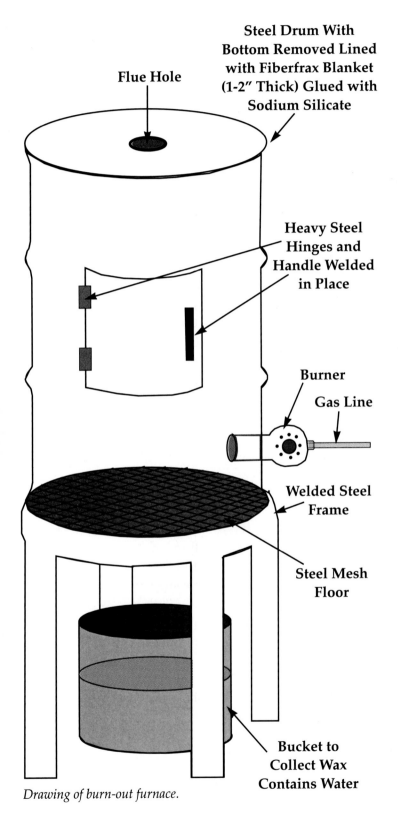

Flue Hole

Steel Drum With Bottom Removed Lined with Fiberfrax Blanket (1-2″ Thick) Glued with Sodium Silicate

Heavy Steel Hinges and Handle Welded in Place

Burner

Gas Line

Welded Steel Frame

Steel Mesh Floor

Bucket to Collect Wax Contains Water

Drawing of burn-out furnace.

The burn out is complete when it stops smoking and all of the carbon residue is gone. A properly fired shell will appear translucent.

Casting hot glass: Preheat the mold to about 1000F. Support the mold in a bed of sand. Ladle or gather glass to fill the mold; when it is full, place it in an annealing oven as quickly as possible. The shell does not retain heat.

Kiln casting: The mold is filled with frit or set up for drip casting like other refractory molds.

Shell removal: After the casting has reached room temperature, support it on a bed of foam rubber and tap gently away from the cast surface with chisel and mallet. The shell should pop off easily.

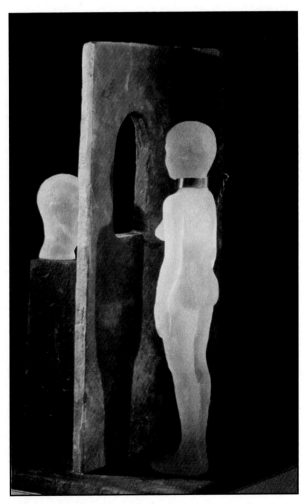

Lucartha Kohler, "Love Story III," figure cast in ceramic shell mold, 1994, glass, brass, 24″ high x 12″ wide x 12″ deep. (photo by the author)

203

Kilns

Kilns come in lots of different shapes and sizes. In fact, a one-time-use kiln can be built for a specific piece of glass to be fired and then disassembled. The best type of kiln for firing glass is an electric kiln. Electric kilns have a constant oxidizing atmosphere, therefore, colors are more stable and heat distribution and temperature changes are more easily controlled.

There are a number of companies making kilns for firing glass (some are listed in "Supply Sources"). Most of these kilns have been designed for fusing and have additional elements in the top. This type of kiln works better for some slumping and most fusing, as there is an even layer of heat directed down on the glass to be fused. Casting prefers heat coming from the bottom and sides to melt the glass in a mold. Ideally, the best placement of elements for casting would be the bottom, because glass fills the mold by heat and gravity. A heat source under the mold would help pull the glass down into the mold cavity.

Any kiln will work, even commercial ceramic kilns work just fine for glass. They are also available in a variety of sizes and styles: both front loading and top loading. Flat glass, even molds may be fired on shelves;

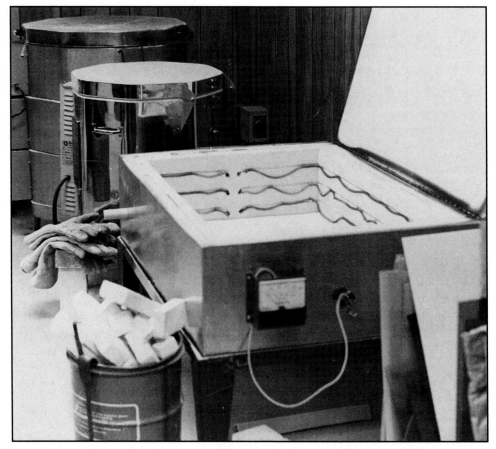

Two commercial ceramic kilns—one hand-built fusing kiln with pyrometer. (photo by the author)

several can be fired at one time. High fire or cone 10 kilns are very good for casting, as they tend to reach casting temperatures more rapidly and the elements tend to last longer, as the maximum firing temperatures for glass are well below the 2500F rating.

Build your own kiln: If the size of commercially available kilns does not correspond with your work, you can build your own. Electric kilns are very simple in design. Like an oversized toaster oven.

A variety of refractory or insulating materials are available for building kilns. Soft firebrick is the least expensive. These bricks can be held in place within a metal frame (do not use galvanized steel as the zinc coating is toxic when it gets hot). More costly is precast refractory ceramic fiber board such as Babcock and Wilcox "Kaowool" M board and Johns Mansville "Marinite" board. All of the refractory companies make similar products. These products' advantage are their lightweight and insulating qualities. Their disadvantage is that once fired they become fragile and shed fibers and dust, which is crystalbolite–a toxic form

Hand-built studio kiln. (photo courtesy the Studio of the Corning Museum of Glass)

of silica. Panels or blocks can be cast from castable insulating refractory materials like A.P. Green's Mazzou, Kast-O-Lite 25 or denser refractory materials like Greencast 97. In any case, a metal frame is needed to support the block and attach the doors and lid.

Another important factor is the thickness of the insulating material. Walls that are too thin will lose heat rapidly, and walls that are too thick will store heat too long. A 3" to 4" thick wall of most refractory materials is sufficient. It's wise to check with the manufacturer of a refractory product to determine the appropriate thickness needed for your particular size and kiln use. Refractory materials are rated to the maximum suggested temperature range, this is sometimes referred to as the K-factor. A refractory material rated for 1000F should not be used to build a kiln to be fired in excess of that temperature, a rating should well exceed the projected firing range. In other words, a K-25 refractory would be rated to 2500F and would be adequate for a 2000F kiln.

Car kiln at Wheaton Village.

Wiring the kiln is the next step. To figure the amount of element wire needed to properly heat the kiln, you need to consider several factors. The principle is simple: an electrical current is run as the main power source to resistance elements and radiant heat is generated. An understanding of the terms involved helps:

Ampere: Unit of intensity of current (measured unit produced by one volt acting through a resistance of 1 ohm).

Ohm: Measured unit of resistance of a conductor (potential of one volt to produce a current of 1 ampere).

Ohms Law: $R = E/I$ (E represents volts; I represents amperes; R represents ohms). To calculate the amount of watts required to heat the kiln, figure 1 to 1-1/2 watts per cubic inch of interior space. Next, to figure the amount of element wire required to produce a given number of watts, you apply Ohms Law, $R = E/I$. For instance, a kiln of 9,000 cubic inches, allowing 1 watt per cubic inch or 9,000 watts; E = 220 volts, I = 30 amps, then R = 7.3. If 18-gauge nichrome wire is used with 0.422 ohms-per-foot resistance and you need 7.3 ohms, then 17.3 feet of wire is required of 1,000-watt element wire. Since you need 9000 watts, then 9 x 1000, or nine elements of 1,000 or three rows of elements; 3 x 17.3 = 51.9 feet long (uncoiled).

Volt: Unit of electrical potential or force (electromotive force steadily applied to a conductor with 1 ohm resistance will produce 1 ampere)

Watts: Unit of power (work of 1 amp under pressure of 1 volt)

The resistance of a conductor depends on its dimensions, temperature and material. Resistance increases as the temperature rises; heavier gauge wire will produce more radiant heat faster. You cannot use heavy gauge wire to heat a small kiln. It is helpful to have an ohm meter to measure the ohm resistance of a given wire. If any two factors of Ohms Law are known, the third can be calculated by using the formula.

Nichrome, a nickel-chrome alloy, is very serviceable for most kilns. More costly kanthal elements will last longer and may be more cost efficient in the long run. The element wire can be coiled by wrapping around a wood dowel. It is also possible to purchase coiled element wire from kiln manufacturers and Duralite (see "Supply Sources" section). When ordering wire, you will need the above information or send them an old element wire. Plugs are rated to amps: a 40-amp three-prong range plug must match a 40-amp receptacle; a 60-amp three-prong plug is slightly different and is known as an arc welder plug. It must have a matching receptacle. Both must have 220-volt service. Higher volt service is more energy efficient.

Element wires must be attached to the kiln walls. Most refractory materials are easily cut; grooves to support the elements are the easiest. The elements can be pinned into the grooves with kanthal or nichrome wire or ceramic element holders. If using wire, take care that the wire pins do not touch the outside metal casing.

Controls or switches are another important consideration. Simple three-stage switches or infinite control switches can be purchased, which mean you turn the kiln on and off. An accurate pyrometer is vital as it is the only means of temperature control. Set-point controllers enable you set a temperature on the dial; when the kiln reaches that temperature, it will hold there until you change it–this is a good design for glassblowing and flame-working annealing ovens. There are many types of programmable temperature control units on the market now. They allow you to enter a program that ramps up to high temperature (slumping, fusing and casting), then ramps down more slowly through an extended annealing cycle. Many commercial kilns now come with them already installed. The most popular one used by glass artists is made by Digitry Co. (see "Supply Sources" section).

Pyrometric cones can be used to measure temperatures. It's a good idea every once in a while to check your pyrometer against a cone system. There are two kinds of cones: standard and junior cones used with a kiln-sitter. They have slightly different temperature ratings so check with the chart to be sure. Standard cones are used three at a time in a wad of clay or a specially designed holder. The center cone is the correct temperature, the one before is lower and the one after is higher. The pad is placed in the kiln so it is visible through peep holes or vents. When the first cone is all the way down and the middle cone bent, but before the higher cone moves, the correct temperature has been reached.

Cone Temperature Conversion

Glass	Cone	Temperature	
Low fire enamels, glass, gold, silver, platinum	022	1112F	600C
Slump soft glass	019	1265F	685C
Slump soft glass	018	1337F	725C
Slump plate glass	017	1386F	752C
Fusing range, soft	016	1443F	784C
Fusing range, glass	015	1485F	807C
Full fuse, soft glass, fuse plate glass	014	1528F	831C
Casting range, lead glasses	011	1623F	884C
Most soft glasses (COE 95 and above)	010	1641F	894C
Soft glass (COE 95 and below)	09	1693F	924C
Bottle glass, some flat glass	08	1751F	955C
Borosilicate glass	07	1803F	984C

Some Kiln Do's and Don'ts

1. Don't fire kilns unattended unless you have a good digital programmer.
2. Don't reach into kiln with out turning it off first.
3. Wear proper clothing and have high temperature gloves when opening kiln at high temperatures.
4. Never burn wax out in kiln. Wax is flammable, toxic and can ruin elements.
5. Have approved electrician do major wiring and power supply.
6. Have adequate ventilation (see "Health Hazards" section).

Annealing

During a demonstration to a group of people, I was explaining the importance of annealing or slow cooling of a glass object to relieve stress. A voice piped up and said "People should be annealed! The term should apply to people, too." Everybody laughed. The idea of slow cooling to reduce stress seemed like a good one to me. It also sums up just what annealing means.

Hot glass, when cooled, is subject to internal stress and strain because it is a super-cooled liquid. As glass cools, the surface contracts first, while the center cools more slowly. This leaves the center under tension. Annealing, the controlled slow-cooling of glass, reduces objectionable permanent and temporary stress. "Stress" equals force-per-unit area and "strain" equals deformation-per-unit length. It is never possible to remove all stress and strain. There is a limit of stress considered acceptable.

Annealing needs not be complicated. Understanding the basic concept of slow and controlled cooling is the first step. To properly anneal any glass it must be very slowly cooled from just above the annealing point to just below the strain point, then slowly cooled from the strain point to room temperature. Glass formulas vary and will differ according to types of glass. Specific glasses are generally referred to by a measurable property known as the coefficient of thermal expansion, or the rate glass expands when heated and contracts when cooled. These numbers do not imply that all other glasses of that specific number will be compatible. Viscosity is also an important property of a given glass. Viscosity means that at a high temperature glass is fluid, but never like water; when it is fluid, it has a low viscosity. Glass at cooler temperatures is less fluid and has a higher viscosity like a jar of very thick honey.

Thermal expansion and viscosity data are available from most manufacturers or distributors of glass. The critical temperatures of any glass for annealing purposes are the strain point and the annealing point. For kiln work, lampworking, blowing and casting, the softening point and working point are also important. Here's an example of a typical soda/lime glass with a coefficient of expansion of 93:

<u>Strain Point</u>	<u>Annealing Point</u>	<u>Softening Point</u>	<u>Working Point</u>
883F	957F	1285F	1841F

The size and shape of the object is also an important factor in calculating an appropriate annealing cycle. Straight even walls or uniform thickness when all sides can cool at an even rate are the easiest. Thick and thin areas combined cause the greatest problem with the greatest stress occurring at the point where they join, the thickest area will try to cool more slowly and continue to contract after the thinner parts of the object are cool. The annealing cycle must be calculated for the thickest part. When casting, mold thickness also enters into the equation, especially in the heat-up rate. The mold can help slow down the cooling process as well; if the mold walls are irregular, the cooling will be uneven. You cannot over-anneal glass. However, if glass is exposed to high temperature heat for a long time, devitrification can occur.

Glass compatibility is another factor in obtaining relatively stress-free glass. If two or more glasses are joined together and are not compatible, no amount of time in an annealing oven will make them fit. It is possible to join glasses of slightly mismatched COEs by adding small amounts of other glass in between layers of base glass and compensating for the direction of tension and compression, especially in blown and flameworked ware. The tolerance in fused and cast work is much more critical. For casting, I recommend using glass that has been tested compatible. The rate of cooling for thick glass is calculated by the cubic-inch and is based on the thickest part of an object.

Annealing Cast Glass

by Dr. Frank E. Woolley
The Studio of The Corning Museum of Glass

Stresses in glass. All common glass objects contain stresses. These can be tensile (pulling apart) and compressive (pushing together). Stresses inside the glass must be balanced–if there is tension in one part, there must be compression in another.

Stresses are thermal or mechanical, depending on what caused them. Thermal stresses are those caused by differences in thermal expansion of various parts of the glass piece. Thermal expansion differences are caused by temperature differences within the casting or by differences in chemical composition (incompatibility). The composition may differ because glasses from different sources have been combined or because of cord in the glass from the melting process. Mechanical stresses are caused by gravity, the mountings, handling and vibration.

Thermal stresses can be temporary or permanent. Temporary thermal stresses only exist while there is a temperature difference within the piece, usually during heating or cooling. Permanent thermal stresses remain in the casting after it reaches room temperature. They are formed as the piece cools from its hot plastic condition to its cold elastic condition.

Why glass breaks. Tensile stress breaks glass: The glass breaks when the glass structure is pulled apart. Glass breaks when the sum of all the stresses (temporary, permanent, thermal, mechanical) exceeds the strength of the glass. Surface flaws (scratches, cracks) or buried stones are needed to start a crack by concentrating the stress. This makes tensile stress at the surface far more dangerous than internal tension because there usually are fewer flaws in the interior. Because cracks can grow slowly, delayed breakage can occur, months or years after the casting is made, at permanent stresses only half as high as the level required to break the piece instantly.

The annealing process. Cooling hot glass produces permanent thermal stresses. Slow cooling produces less stress, but all glass has some permanent stress. Annealing is a heat

212

treatment applied to glass to reduce permanent surface tensile stresses to a level that will not significantly contribute to breakage, even when combined for long times with stresses of other types.

If the glass is cooled uniformly on all surfaces, then the surfaces will be left with compressive stress and the center (the region that cools last) will have tensile stress.

The critical temperature range for developing permanent thermal stress is between the *annealing point* and *strain point* of the glass. These temperatures are properties of the glass composition and are not affected by the shape of the casting. Annealing can only reduce stress caused by temperature differences within a casting. Stress caused by incompatibility is not reduced by annealing.

Practical annealing is aimed at preventing immediate and delayed breakage. It is not necessary to remove all permanent thermal stress, but only to reduce it to the point that when combined with mechanical and temporary thermal stresses the piece is unlikely to break. An acceptable level of permanent stress thus depends on the application. It needs to be low if other high stresses will be encountered, as with tableware or outdoor sculpture; it can be higher if the piece is unlikely to be subjected to high stresses, such as indoor decorative articles.

The ideal annealing schedule achieves this adequately low permanent stress level in the shortest time and at the lowest cost. In many cases, it is impractical to try to determine the ideal annealing schedule. The additional cost of a slightly longer schedule is often quite small compared with the risk of breakage if the schedule is too short.

Annealing schedules: Annealing schedules for castings consist of three stages. After cooling from the casting temperature as rapidly as possible to avoid devitrification, the casting is held at a temperature near the annealing point of the glass. This hold allows the entire casting to come to nearly the same temperature. The most critical part of the anneal comes next, when the casting is slowly cooled at a rate selected to produce an acceptable stress level. This slow cool rate is continued until the interior of the glass is below the strain point of the glass. Below this temperature, only temporary stress is created, so the cooling rate can be increased to save time.

The ideal annealing schedule for a piece of glass depends primarily on the thickness and coefficient of thermal expansion (CTE) of the glass, and on the acceptable permanent stress level. It depends secondarily on the glass viscosity (annealing and strain points). If the properties of the glass are known precisely and if the glass is homogeneous, then a schedule can be calculated that will leave the piece with an acceptable permanent stress in the shortest possible time. Frequently, the properties are only known approximately, and the glass is somewhat cordy or is made up of several slightly different glasses. In these cases, it is better to use a somewhat slower schedule to avoid breakage.

The "Annealing Schedules for Casting Glasses" chart shows generic schedules that can be used for castings when the thermal expansion and annealing and strain temperatures are only known approximately. For these conditions, it is practical to use a conservative schedule that will give an adequate anneal without complicated calculations.

Permanent stress is the sum of stress caused by temperature differences during cooling, plus that caused by local differences in thermal expansion due to cord. These generic schedules assume that the glass is somewhat cordy. If your glass has little cord, you could safely cool at rates twice as fast as these schedules. With severely cordy glass, it is impossible to predict the stress caused by the cord. The best approach is to change the source of glass or the casting process to reduce the amount of cord.

These generic schedules are calculated to work for any normal casting glasses of the soda-lime or lead families of compositions. The stress remaining after annealing was calculated for a theoretical worst case, a hypothetical glass that combines the most unfavorable properties found among these two families of glasses:

1. Highest expansion (CTE 110)
2. Highest annealing point (990F or 532C)
3. Lowest strain point (734F or 390C)

For thicker castings, the generic schedule becomes so long that it is better to calculate a more efficient schedule based on the actual properties of the glass you are using.

How to use the annealing tables

Cooling path length (CPL): The stresses that are created during cooling through the strain point are proportional to the temperature difference between the glass surface and the hottest part of the interior. This temperature difference is determined by the cooling rate of the outside surface, and the distance heat must flow from the interior to the surface. For a slab, heat only flows along one axis, perpendicular to the two surfaces. For more realistic shapes, heat may flow in all directions. We want to determine the spot in the piece that will cool last; we will call this the "hot spot." The CPL is half the thickness of a uniform slab whose center will cool the same as the hot spot in your complex casting. For a long cylindrical shape cooled equally over its surface, the hot spot is along the axis and the CPL is about one-fourth the diameter. For a sphere, the CPL is about one-sixth the diameter. Treat a rectangular bar that is more than twice as wide as it is thick as a slab of the same thickness.

To use the "Annealing Schedules for Casting Glasses," imagine your casting as a combination of slabs, cylinders or spheres. Then estimate the CPL using the above guidelines. For example, if your piece is roughly a sphere 6" in diameter with a 4" diameter cylinder protruding from the side, the hot spot will be roughly in the middle of the sphere, and it will have a CPL of about 1". As another example, if your piece is roughly a block 4" thick x 8" wide x 12" long, its CPL of 2" is based only on its thickness. If is only 6" wide, its CPL will be less than that of a large 4" slab, but more than a 4" cylinder: 1.5" would be a reasonable estimate.

Effect of molds. If the glass casting is in a mold during annealing, then heat loss is slowed by the mold. This does not change the cooling rate that is needed, but it can have a major effect on the location of the hot spot and on the location of the tensile stresses.

The thermal conductivity of plaster-based molds is roughly one-third that of glass at annealing temperatures. To estimate the CPL, imagine your casting surrounded by glass three times thicker than the mold on each face. Then apply the guidelines above to determine its hot spot. The CPL is now the distance from the hot spot to the actual surface of the casting through which heat will be lost. For example, if we are annealing a block 4" thick x 8" wide x 12" long in an open-faced mold 3″ thick with the 8″ by 12″ face exposed, the hot spot is found by adding an imaginary 9″ of glass to the sides of the casting that contact the mold. This gives an imaginary casting 13″ thick x 26″ wide x 30″ long. It loses heat like a large slab 13″ thick in which the hot spot is 6.5″ from the exposed surface and the CPL is 6.5″. That means that the actual hot spot will be in the plaster mold, and the embedded face of the casting will be left in tension. Even using an annealing schedule for a 6.5″ slab, the surface tensile stress will invite breakage. This example illustrates two important rules for castings annealed in molds:

1. If the mold is the same thickness on all sides of the casting, it can be ignored in selecting the annealing schedule.
2. If the mold is open, the CPL will be at least the actual total thickness of the piece, and the annealing schedule will be at least four times longer.

The extremely long schedules required by open molds can be avoided by simply covering the open face with insulating board or blanket. If the insulation has the same thermal resistance as the mold, then the hot spot will be moved back to the center of the piece and the CPL will drop to half the thickness of the piece.

Importance of uniform temperature in the annealer. The temperature differences within a casting during the slow cooling stage are typically only a few degrees. If your annealer has comparable temperature differences from one end to the other or from the center to the door, then stresses may be developed that are as large as the permanent stress from annealing. In addition, the tensile stress will be located wherever the casting cooled last, so one end or face of the casting will be left in tension. Clearly, it is important to have a uniform temperature within the annealer. Tight-fitting doors and circulating fans are very helpful.

Annealing Schedules for Casting Glasses

(Conservative schedules for all soda-lime and lead glasses)

	Soak Step		Slow Cool Step					Fast Cool to Room Temperature				
Cooling path length	Soak temp.	Soak time	Slow cool temp. change	Slow cool rate	Slow cool time	End slow cool temp.	Total time to end of slow cool	Fast cool temp. change	Fast cool rate	Fast cool time	Total time to end of fast cool	
inches	degrees F	hr	degrees F	degrees F per hr	hr	degrees F	hr	degrees F	degrees F per hr	hr	hr	days
0.50	990	0.2	296	79	3.8	694	4.0	624	314	2.0	6.0	0.2
1.00	985	0.8	291	20	14.8	694	15.6	624	79	7.9	23.5	1.0
1.50	980	2	286	8.7	33	694	35	624	35	18	52	2.2
2.00	975	3	281	4.9	57	694	60	624	20	32	92	3.8
3.00	970	7	276	2.2	126	694	134	624	8.7	72	205	8.5
4.00	970	13	276	1.23	225	694	237	624	4.9	127	365	15
5.00	970	20	276	0.79	351	694	371	624	3.1	199	570	24
6.00	970	29	276	0.55	505	694	534	624	2.2	286	820	34

This schedule is based on the following glass properties:
Coefficient of thermal expansion–110 x 10^-7/degrees Celsius
Coefficient of thermal expansion–0C-300C
Annealing point–990F; 532C
Strain point–734F; 390C
No actual glass has these properties. In general, a shorter schedule can be calculated if the actual glass properties are known.

Health Hazards

A real concern for artists working in glass is the safe handling of materials and equipment in the studio. Many of the materials used can be dangerous if not handled properly; careless use of equipment can cause serious accidents.

Good **hot glass studio** design should include a proper exhaust system vented out of the building to remove carbon monoxide, gas fumes and toxic elements from the furnace and glory hole. It should also have a hood with exhaust to remove excess dust from glass powders and fuming techniques. NIOSH-approved respirators should be worn when handling batch and refractory materials, as well as grinding, polishing and sandblasting. Eye protection is important from ultraviolet and infrared radiation. Proper clothing is essential. No loose-fitting garments that can get caught on equipment or come in contact with hot glass. Do not wear synthetic fibers, because they can catch on fire, melt and stick to your skin. Cotton work clothes are best. Burns are a big problem. Molten glass is between 2000F and 2400F. It stays hot for a long time. Equipment used to shape glass also stays hot a long time. Non-asbestos fire-proof gloves should be worn when transferring ware to annealing ovens or coming in direct contact with the glass, especially casting hot glass.

Flameworking shares many of the same protective measures as glassblowing. A hood with a proper exhaust system over the torch is very important. A number of toxic gasses are produced by melting the glass with a torch, plus the carbon monoxide caused by gas burning oxygen can build up undetected. Eye protection is essential. Didymium glasses protect the eyes from ultraviolet radiation and filter the glare from molten glass. Looking at a torch is very much like looking directly at the sun at noon in midsummer. Burns can be avoided by simple measures and good work habits. Never reach in front of the torch; pay attention to where hot ends of rods are placed and heat glass slowly in the torch to avoid ends popping off into your face.

Kilnworking involves many processes and each has a different set of precautions. Kilns require a good exhaust system vented to the outdoors. Fumes should be vented from the natural and chemical water released from the molds. Toxic gasses can be released from some glasses at elevated temperatures. Clay kiln wash, refractory materials, mold materials and finely ground glass powders all contain silica dust. Fumes caused by burning wax are toxic. Wax should be steamed or melted from a mold at a low temperature. Some rubber mold materials give off toxic fumes and should be handled accordingly.

Many **surface decorating** techniques involve toxic chemicals or hazardous dusts. Fired metallics and glass enamels contain metal oxides and an oil or lacquer binder which, if not toxic, are unpleasant to smell. Hydrofluoric acid is very dangerous and can be fatal.

Cold working, cutting, grinding, polishing carving, sawing and sandblasting all present the problem of silica dust. When the slurry powders from the machining of glass dry, the particles can become airborne and present a dust hazard. Whenever possible, aluminum oxide or silicon carbide should be used as an abrasive, as they have less adverse effects on health. Silicone and plastic adhesives can produce contact dermatitis, while long-time exposure can cause severe allergic reactions in some people.

Elements and Health Risks

Cadmium: Chronic inhalation may cause kidney damage, anemia, gastrointestinal problems and is a possible carcinogen.

Chromium: Chronic inhalation is a possible carcinogen.

Cobalt: Chronic inhalation may cause asthma.

Lead: Lead poisoning can effect gastrointestinal system, anemia, brain damage, neuromuscular system, birth defects during pregnancy

Manganese: Chronic inhalation can affect the nervous system causing a disease resembling Parkinson's Disease.

Selenium: Chronic inhalation may cause respiratory irritation.

Sodium cyanide: Extremely toxic. Inhalation, ingestion and skin contact can be fatal.

Toxic oxides: When oxides used as colorants vaporize during the melting or firing process, the inhalation risk is high.

Uranium: Chronic inhalation may cause emphysema or lung cancer, due to radioactivity.

Hazardous Dusts/Particles Health Risks

Asbestos: Chronic inhalation or general exposure can cause cancer.

Plaster: Slightly irritating to eyes and respiratory system. Chronic inhalation may cause more severe respiratory problems. Thermo-set reaction may cause burns to skin.

Pumice: Contains silica.

Silica: Chronic inhalation causes silicosis, a painful lung disease caused by silica dust particles entering the lungs. Scar tissue is formed around the particle and continues to grow. There is no reversal of the process or cure for silicosis. There are three types of crystalline forms of silica: quartz, cristobalite and tridymite. Silica is found in many materials: clay, glazes, flint, glass, pumice, sand and refractory materials. Refractory ceramic fibers are partially converted to cristobalite one of the more toxic forms of silica. It is a possible carcinogen.

Vermiculite: Contains asbestos, possible carcinogen.

Zircon: Chronic inhalation may cause allergic reactions in nasal passages. May contain free silica.

Chemicals and Health Risks

Hydrochloric acid: Contact is highly corrosive to skin, stomach and lungs.

Hydrofluoric acid: Contact is highly corrosive to skin, stomach and lungs. Can be fatal.

Plastics and polymers: Some of the plastic adhesives such as epoxies and ultraviolet glues can cause allergic reactions. Long-time exposure can cause severe dermatitis.

Silicones: Contain acetic acid which is highly irritating to eyes and respiratory system.

In addition, be careful with solvents. Although this list reads like a doom and gloom forecast, all of these materials except asbestos can be used if the proper safety measures are followed. *Respirators, dust masks, safety glasses and prudent work habits contribute to a safe working environment.*

Supply Sources

Adhesives

Conservators Emporium: 100 Standing Rock Cir., Reno, NV 89511, (702) 825-0404; Hyxtal.

Dewey Associates: 459 Main St., Ste. 102, New Rochelle, NY, (914) 633-4081, 800-448-2306; Dymax UV, light sources.

HIS Glassworks, Inc.: 91 Webb Cove Rd., Asheville, NC, (704) 254 2559, 800-914-7462; Hyxtal and UV glue.

Locktite Corp.: call 800-562-0560 for nearest distributor; Locktite UV, light sources.

Norland Products Inc.: 695 Joyce Kilmer Ave., New Brunswick, NJ 08902, 908-545-7828; UV glues and light sources.

Spectronics Corp.: P.O. Box 483, Westbury, NY 11590, 516-333-4840; UV light sources.

Ceramic Shell

Johnson Atelier Sculpture Supplies: 50 Princeton-Heightstown Rd., Ste. L, Princeton Junction, NJ 08550, 800-732-7203.

Ransom and Randolf: (see under "Mold Material-Refractory").

Decorating

Acheson Colloids Co.: P.O. Box 611747, Port Huron, MI 48061-1747, (313) 984-5581; Electro-dag for electroplating.

AMACO: 4717 W 16 St., Indianapolis, IN 46209; glass enamels.

Paradise Paints: 2902 Neal Rd., Paradise, CA, 95969, (916) 872-5020; high-fire enamels.

Peacock Laboratories: 54th St. & Paschall Ave., Philadelphia, PA 19143, (215) 729-4400; mirroring supplies.

Reusche: 1299 H St., Greeley, CO 80631; (970) 346-8577, glass enamels.

Safer Solutions: (215) 232-5459

Standard Ceramic Supply Co.: P.O. Box 4435, Pittsburgh, PA, (412) 923-1655; glass enamels.

Thompson Enamels: P.O. Box 314, Kellville, KY 41072, (606) 291-3800; glass enamels, Klyr-fire.

Glass

Blenko Glass Co.: Milton, WV 25541, (304) 743-9081; flat glass, chunks, slabs.

C and R Loo: 1085 Essex Ave., Richmond, CA 94801, 800-227-1780; complete source.

Bullseye Glass Co.: 3722 S.E. 21st Ave., Portland, OR 97202, (503) 232-8887; flat glass, frit available through stained glass distributors.

Fritworks: c/o Anna Booth, P.O. Box 158, Zeiglerville, PA 19492-0158, (610) 287-0221.

S.A. Bendheim Co. Inc.: 122 Hudson St., New York, NY 10013, 800-225-7379; flat glass, frit, fusing supplies.

Hudson Glass: 219 N. Division St., Peekskill, NY, 800-431-2964; flat glass, frit, fusing supplies.

Schott Glass: 400 York Ave., Durea, PA 18642, (717) 457-7485.

Other: Local stained glass suppliers, local plate and mirror glass companies–check area phone directories.

Kilns

Jen-Ken Kilns: 3615 Ventura Dr., W. Lakeland, FL 33811, (813) 648-0585; glass kilns.

Denver Glass Machine Inc.: 2800 S. Shoshone, Englewood, CO 80110, (303) 781-0980.

Olympic Kilns: 6301 Button Gwinnett Dr., Atlanta, GA 30340.

Digitry Co.: 108 High St., Portland, ME 04102, (207) 774-0300; digital programmer.

Duralite: P.O. Box 188, Riverton, CT 06065, (203) 379-3113; kiln elements.

Joppa Glassworks, Inc.: P.O. Box 202, Warner, NH 03278, (603) 456-3569; kiln elements.

Lampworking Supplies

Frantz Bead Co. Inc.: E. 1222 Sunset Hill Rd., Shelton, WA 98584, 800-839-6712; bead and lampworking supplies.

Wale Apparatus: 400 Front St., Hellertown, PA 18055, 800-444-Wale; lampworking supplies.

Mold Material-Miscellaneous

Cementex Latex Corp.: 480 Canal St., NY, NY, 800-782-9056; latex mold materials.

Dux Sales: 600 E. Hueneme Rd., Oxnard, CA 93033, 800-833-8267; dental alginate.

Johnson Atelier Sculpture Supplies: (see address under "Ceramic Shell"); dental alginate.

Polytek: 55 Hilton St., Easton, PA 18042, (610) 559-8620; rubber mold materials.

Smooth-On Inc.: 1000 Valley Rd., Gillete, NJ 07933, (908) 647-5800; rubber mold materials.

Synair: P.O. Box 5269, Chattanooga, TN 37406, 800-251-7642; rubber molds.

Texas Art Supply: 2001 Montrose, Houston, TX 77006, (713) 526-5221; Gelflex polyvinyl mold material.

Weaver Industries: 313 Franklin St., Denver, PA 17517, (215) 267-7507; graphite.

Mold Material-Plaster/Silica (200 mesh flint)

Building supply companies: plaster of Paris, gauging plaster, moulding plaster–check area phone directories.

Ceramic supply companies: flint, pottery plaster, kaolin clay.

Mold Material-Refractory

AP Green Refractories Co.: Green Boulevard, Mexico, MO 65265, (314) 473-3626; Cast-O-Lite 24, M board, line of denser castable refractories. Check area phone directories for local distributor.

JH France: Conshohocken, PA, (215) 279-6690 (ask for Stanley); Hydrocon 24, dura board.

Ransom and Randolf: 3535 Briarfield Blvd., Maumee, OH 43537, 800-800-7496.

United Erie Inc.: Erie, PA 16512, (814) 456-7561; gasbond.

Whip Mix Corp.: 361 Farmington Ave., Louisville, KY 40217, 800-626-5651; Cristobolite.

Zircar Products Inc.: P.O. Box 458, Florida, NY 10921, (914) 651-4481; RSDD, RS-100, LCP, Mold Mix 6.

Other: Babcock and Wilcox, North American Refractories, Carborundum–check area phone directories under "Refractories."

Sandblasting

Glass Image: 1932 Valley View Ln., Farmers Branch, TX 75234, 800-628-5254; photo resist.

Granite City Tool Co.: 11 Blackwell St., Barre, VT 05641, (802) 476-3137; sandblast resist, sandblasters.

Main Tape Corp.: P.O. Box 379, Plymouth, WI 53073, 800-858-0481; sandblast resist.

Tip Tools and Equipment: P.O. Box 649, Canfield, OH 44406-9984; all types of sandblasters, resists and safety gear.

Tubelite Co.: 300 Park St., Moonachie, NJ 07074, (201) 641-1011; sandblast resist.

Tools and Equipment

Anchor Tools: P.O. Box 265, Chatham, NJ 07928, (908) 245-7888; glassblowing equipment, diamond bits.

Covington Engineering Corp.: P.O. Box 35, Redlands, CA 92373-0006, (909) 793-6636; saws, grinding and polishing equipment.

Crystalite Corporation: P.O. Box 6127, Westerville, OH 43086-6127, 800-777-2894; diamond wheels, discs, burrs and drills.

Denver Glass Machine Inc.: 2800 S. Shoshone, Englewood, CO 80110, (303) 781-0980; diamond saws, electric furnaces, electric kilns.

Diamond Pro Unlimited: P.O. Box 25, Monteray Park, CA 91754, (818) 281-2277; diamond burrs.

Foredom Electric Co.: Bethel, CT 06801, (203) 792-8622; flex shaft.

Glastar Corp.: 20721 Marilla St., Chatsworth, CA 91311, 800-423-5635; diamond tools.

HIS Glassworks, Inc.: (see address under "Adhesives"); diamond laps.

Lunzer Industrial Diamonds: 280 N. Midland, Saddlebrook, NJ 07663, 800-864-5555; diamond engraving tools.

Sommer & Maca: 5501 W. Ogden Ave., Chicago, IL, 60650, (312) 242-2871; tools, miscellaneous supplies.

Starlite Ind.: 1111 Lancaster Ave., Rosemont, PA, (215) 527-1300; diamond burrs and bits.

Steinert Industries: 1507 Franklin Ave., Kent, OH 44240, 800-727-7473; glassblowing tools, cullet crusher.

Tempo Glove Mfg. Inc.: 3820 W. Wisconsin Ave., Milwaukee, WI 53208; 800-558-8520.

Trow and Holden: 45 S. Main St., Barre, VT 05641, 800-451-4349; pneumatic and electrical diamond tools and chisels for stone and glass.

Wale Apparatus: (see address under "Lampworking Supplies"); lampworking supplies, diamond burrs, drill bits, gloves, etc.

Wax

Kindt-Collins Co.: 12651 Elmwood Ave., Cleveland, OH 44111, 800-321-3170; wax.

Walnut Hill Enterprises Inc.: P.O. Box 599, Bristol, PA 19007, (215) 785-6511; wax.

Miscellaneous

Edmund Scientific Company: 101 East Gloucester Pike, Barrington, NJ 08007-1380, (609) 547-8880; polarized film, optics, lasers, prisms, lots of great stuff.

Sepp Leaf Products: 381 Park Ave. South, New York, NY 10016, (212) 683-2840.

Dick Blick: art supplies, P.O. Box 1267, Galesburg, Ill 61401, 800-447-8192, (309) 343-6181.

Pearl Paint: art supplies catalog, mail order 800-221-6845, Ext. 2297.

Publications

American Craft: 72 Spring St., NY 10012, (212) 274-0630.

Glass Magazine: Urban Glass, 647 Fulton St., Brooklyn, NY 11217, (718) 625-3685.

Glass Art: P.O. Box 260377, Highlands Ranch, CO 80126, (303) 791-8998.

Neus Glas: 1850 Union St. #228, San Francisco, CA 94123, (415) 441-0629.

Societies

Glass Art Society: 1305 4th Ave. Ste. 711, Seattle, WA 98101-2401, (206) 382-1305.

Bibliography

Artist Beware, 2nd ed., Michal McCann, Ph.D., Watson-Guptil, NY: 1992.

The Art of Painting on Glass, Albinas Elskus, Charles Scribner's Sons, NY: 1980.

The Artist's Complete Health and Safety Guide, Monona Rossol, Allworth Press, NY: 1992.

Alternative Photographic Processes, Kent E. Wade, Morgan & Morgan Inc., Dobbs Ferry, NY: 1978.

Annealing and Strengthening in the Glass Industry, Dr. Alexis G. Pincus, Thomas R. Holmes, publisher, Books for Industry and the Glass Industry, Magazines for Industry, NY.

Ed's Big Handbook of Glassblowing, Glass Mountain Press, Jamestown, CO: 1993, 1997.

Ceramic Industry, Cahner's Publication, Vol. #108, #1 January 1977.

Coloured Glasses, Woldemar A. Weyl, Society of Glass Technology, Sheffield, England: reprinted 1992.

The Complete Book of Silk Screen Printing Production, J.I. Biegeleisen, Dover Publisher, NY: 1963.

A Complete Guide to Printmaking, edited by Stephen Russ, Viking Press: 1975.

Contemporary Glass: A World Survey from The Corning Museum of Glass, Susanne K. Frantz, Harry N. Abroms, NY: 1989.

Contemporary Lampworking, Bandhu Scott Dunham, Salusa Glass works, Arizona: 1994.

Copyart, Patrick Firpo, Lester Alexander, Claudia Katayanagi, Horseguard Lane Productions, Ltd., Richard Marek, publisher, NY: 1980.

Contemporary Art Glass, Ray and Lee Grover, Crown Publisher, NY: 1975.

Creative Glass Blowing, James E. Hammesfahr, Clair L. Strong, W.H. Freeman and Co., San Francisco.

Cut and Engraved Glass, Dorothy Daniel, M. Barrows and Co. Inc.: 1966.

Daum Maitres Verriers, Edita Denol, Denoel Publisher, France.

De Re Metalica, Georgius Agricola, translated Herbert Clark Hoover and Lou Henry Hoover,* Dover Publisher: 1950.

Dictionary of Glass: Materials and Techniques, Charles Bray, London, A&C Black, Philadelphia, University of Pennsylvania Press: 1995.

Electroplating and Electroforming for Artists and Craftsmen, Lee Scott Newman and Jay Hartley Newman, Crown Publisher, NY: 1979.

5000 Years of Glass, Hugh Tait, Harry N. Abroms, NY: 1991.

English Looking Glasses, Geoffrey Wills, A.S. Barnes and Co., London: 1965.

Flameworking, Frederick Schuler, Chilton Book Co., Philadelphia: 1968.

Glass: Art Nouveau to Art Deco, Victor Arwas, Rizzoli International, NY: 1977.

Glass: A Contemporary Art, Dan Klein, Rizzoli International, NY: 1989.

Glass: A Pocket Dictionary of Terms Commonly Used to Describe Glass and Glassmaking, David Whitehouse, The Corning Museum of Glass, Corning, NY.

Glassblowing, Frank Kulasiewicz, Watson-Guptil, NY: 1974.

Glassblowing, A Search for Form, Harvey K. Littleton, Van Nostrand Reinhold Co., NY: 1971.

Glass Engineering Handbook, E.B. Shand, McGraw-Hill Book Co., NY: 1958.

Glass Engraving, Barbara Norman, Arco Publisher: 1981.

Glassforming, Frederick Schuler and Lilli Schuler, Chilton Book Co., Philadelphia: 1970.

Glass, Philosophy and Method, John Burton, Bonanza Books, NY: 1967.

Glass Notes, Henry Halem, Halem Studios, Inc., Kent, OH: 1993.

The Glass of Frederick Carder, Paul Gardner, Crown Publisher, NY: 1971.

Gold Leaf Techniques, third edition by Kent H. Smith, Signs of the Times Publishing Co., Cincinnati: 1992.

The History of Glass, Dan Klein and Lloyd Ward, ed., Orbis, London.

An Illustrated Dictionary of Glass, Harold Newman, Thames and Hudson: 1977.

Innovative Printmaking, Thelma R. Newman Crown, NY: 1977.

Kilns: Design, Construction and Operation, Daniel Rhodes, Chilton Book Co., Philadelphia: 1968.

Making Glass Beads, Cindy Jenkins, Lark Books, Asheville, NC: 1979.

Masterpieces of American Glass, The Corning Museum, Jane Shaddel Spillman and Susanne K Frantz, Toledo Museum, Lillian Nassau, Crown, NY: 1990.

More than You Ever Wanted to Know About Glass Beadmaking, Glass Wear Studios, Livermore CA: 1995.

On Divers Arts, John G. Hawthorne and Cyril, Stanley Smith, Dover Publisher: 1979.

Pate de verre and Kiln Casting of Glass, Jim Kervin and Dan Fenton, Glass Wear Studios, Livermore CA: 1997.

Properties of Glass and Glass Ceramics, Corning Bulletin.

A Short History of Glass, Chloe Zerwick, Harry N. Abroms, NY: 1990.

Studio Glassmaking, Ray Flavell and Claude Smale, Van Nostrand Reinhold, NY: 1974.

Techniques of Kiln Formed Glass, Keith Cummings, A&C Black, London, University of Pennsylvania Press, Philadelphia: 1997.

Visual Art in Glass, Dominick Labino, William Brown Company, Dubuque, IA: 1968.

Glossary

Acid polish: Polishing or frosting by dipping in hydrochloric and or sulfuric acids. (dangerous endeavor)**

Alumina hydrate: Refractory powder used as a separator between glass and kiln shelf or clay and metal molds.**

Anneal: Slow and gradual cooling of glass from higher working temperatures to room temperature to reduce the amount of stress inherent in all types of glass.

Annealing oven: Refractory chamber used for annealing blown and lampworked glass and for firing slumped, fused and cast glass objects, as well as vitreous enamels and lusters.

Asbestos: Refractory material made from chrysolite fibers. (causes cancer)**

Batch: Sand, soda and lime mixed with coloring oxides to be melted in a glass furnace.**

Bead: Round ball, usually with a hole in the center, formed by winding molten glass around a wire. The tendency of glass is to form a round ball when heated.

Bentonite: Extremely plastic material formed by volcanic ash often used in clay bodies. Bonds sand particles together for sand casting.

Cane: Rod of glass usually pulled from a large gather of hot glass; nowadays, most often machine made. Canes are used to deco rate blown glass objects and with a torch to make scientific apparatus, novelties and glass beads.

Casting: Process of making a positive form using a mold.

Check: Cracks in a glass object often caused by glass incompatibility or an inaccurate annealing cycle.

Cire perdue: French term for lost wax casting process.

Chemical water: Water chemically combined in plaster and clay molds. This water will evaporate at approximately 800F.

Coefficient of expansion: Ratio of change between the length of a material mass and the temperature; or the rate glass expands and contracts when heated and cooled. It's very important when combining different types of glasses hot that the coefficient of expansion match.

Cullet: Glass left over from previous melts.

Decal: Special paper on which designs are printed with glass enamels to be transferred to a glass object before firing.

Devitrification: Formation of crystals in glass, usually found on the surface of a glass that has been held at elevated temperatures. Looks hazy!

Divestment: Process of removing a casting from its mold when cooled.

Dichroic: Thin film of metal coating on glass, applied by a vacu-forming process. Reflects light differently on each side.

Enamels: Low-melting glass powders mixed with a resin or oil binder used to decorate glass. Can be painted, air brushed or silk-screened.

Engraving: Process of carving a design on the surface of a glass object with diamond tools or copper wheels.

Etching: Process of patterning a glass object, usually by acid or abrasive blasting.

Flashing: Excess material caused by mold fissures and mold seams that requires grinding.

Flint-silica flour: Used in glaze formulation and molds for casting, 200 mesh or 380 mesh**

Flux: Low-melting compounds such as lead, borox, soda or lime. The flux combines with silica to lower the melting temperature of pure silica (3000F) in the manufacture of glass.

Frit: Glass that has been melted then broken into small pieces by dropping in water. Often used for pate de verre or kiln casting.

Fuse: Bonding or melting together different pieces of compatible glass by means of heat.

Glass: Rigid liquid made from a mixture of oxides. Some oxides act as a flux and lower the melting temperature of the glass. Soft glasses such as lead glass and soda/lime melt at a low temperature. "Pyrex" or borosilicate glass and quartz glasses melt at a higher temperature and are called hard glasses.

Glassblowing: Glass gathered on the end of a blowpipe and formed into a variety of shapes by blowing air through the blowpipe into the molten glass.

Gather: Glass collected on the end of a blowpipe or punty from a glass furnace.

Glory hole: Secondary furnace used to reheat glass in the glass blowing procedure.

Gums: Arabic or tragacanth, natural resins used as water soluble binders for glass enamels.

Investment: Refractory material used in making molds for casting glass or metals.

Iridescence: Luster effect caused by spraying hot glass with chlorides or nitrates of metals such as tin and silver.**

Kiln: Chamber made from refractory material for the purpose of firing ceramics and glass.

Kiln forming: Glass that is shaped in an electric or gas kiln by casting, fusing or slumping.

Kiln elements: Coiled high temperature wire used to heat kiln chamber. Wires must be rated according to amps and volts of a kiln.

Kiln sitter: Shut-off device using pyrometric cones calibrated to specific temperatures relative to firing glass and ceramics.

Kiln wash: a refractory powder mixed with water and applied to kiln shelves, clay and metal molds and bead mandrels to prevent glass from fusing to them.**

Kaolin: Ball clay or china clay, often used as ingredient in kiln wash or mandrel release for beadmaking.

Lehr: Oven used for annealing glass. Term most often used in the glass industry.

Lost wax casting: Casting process using a refractory mold over a wax positive, then the wax is steamed or burned out, leaving a cavity for ladling molten glass or filling with frit for kiln casting.

Lusters: Metallic oxides in a resin binder deposit a thin coating of metal on a glass surface when fired.**

Mandrel: Term used in glass bead making to describe the wire or rod around which a bead is wound.

Marver: Heavy flat plate usually of steel,(was at one time marble hence the name),It is used to cool and shape glass during the blowing process

Millefiori: Means a thousand flowers. Glass rods made by bundling many smaller rods into a pattern.

Mold: Negative form into which glass is blown, slumped or cast.

Oxides: Compound of an element and oxygen used as ingredients in glass. Metal oxides add color; for instance, iron oxide makes green, cobalt makes blue and gold makes ruby glass.**

Pate de verre: Means paste of glass. Kiln casting process in which a paste of finely crushed glass is pressed into a mold and fired. The term sometimes refers to all kiln cast glass.

Plaster (of Paris): Hydrate of calcium sulfate. Hardens when mixed with water. Ideal mold for casting glass when mixed with silica flour.**

Polariscope: Optical device used to show stress in glass. Uses two pieces of polarized film at right angles to each other.

Punty or pontil: Solid rod, usually stainless steel, used to finish blown glass objects or to form solid objects such as paper weights.

Pyrometer: Instrument for measuring heat, consisting of a temperature gauge connected by wire to a thermocouple, inserted through a hole into an oven to give an accurate reading of the heat chamber.

Pyrometric cones: Small triangular ceramic cones that are made to bend at specific temperatures to indicate the internal temperature of an oven. There are witness cones and junior cones, the latter are used in an automatic shut-off device called a kiln sitter.

Resists: Film or wax used to resist the action of sand blasting, acid etching, photo process or printing with enamels.

Respirator: Mask covering the nose and mouth to filter dusts and hazardous vapors. It's very important to the have the proper filters.

Sandblasting: Abrasive blast process that propels grit under pressure through a gun to abrade the surface of a glass object.

Sand carving: Abrasive blast process that carves deeply into the surface of a glass object

Sand casting: Process of hot casting glass by ladling molten glass from a furnace into a negative impression made in damp sand or chemically bonded sand.

Silica: Sand, raw material used in glassmaking, refractory materials, glazes and as an ingredient in casting molds.**

Sodium Silicate: Water-soluble binder for refractory molds, often referred to as water glass.

Softening point: Temperature above the annealing point of a specific glass when it will begin to deform under its own weight.

Slumping: Glass that has been shaped with heat and gravity by bending over or into a mold. Sometimes called bent or sagged glass.

Strain point: Point of a given glass when the internal stresses are significantly reduced. At this point, the glass is rigid. Under cut an

area of a positive or negative form that prevents easy
removal from a mold.

Whiting: Calcium carbonate, a fine refractory powder used in kiln wash.

Zircon: Fine refractory powder non-wetting to glass.**

** Use proper safety precautions when handling.

References

1. Hutchins, J.R. III, and R.V. Harrington, The American Society for Testing and Materials, Glass, Corning Glass Works, reprinted from Kirk-Othmer: *Encyclopedia of Chemical Technology*, 2nd ed., Volume 10, 1966, John Wiley & Sons, 1966, p.534.
2. © 1978 Lucartha Kohler

Index

Photo Index